WORLD RELIGIONS

ZOROASTRIANISM
THIRD EDITION

WORLD RELIGIONS

African Traditional Religion
Baha'i Faith
Buddhism
Catholicism & Orthodox Christianity
Confucianism
Daoism
Hinduism
Islam
Judaism
Native American Religions
Protestantism
Shinto
Sikhism
Zoroastrianism

WORLD RELIGIONS
ZOROASTRIANISM
THIRD EDITION

by
Paula R. Hartz
Series Editors: Joanne O'Brien and Martin Palmer

CHELSEA HOUSE
PUBLISHERS
An imprint of Infobase Publishing

Zoroastrianism, Third Edition

Chelsea House
An imprint of Infobase Publishing
132 West 31st Street
New York NY 10001

Library of Congress Cataloging-in-Publication Data
Hartz, Paula.
 Zoroastrianism / by Paula R. Hartz. – 3rd ed.
   p. cm. — (World religions)
 Includes bibliographical references and index.
 ISBN 978-1-60413-116-1
 1. Zoroastrianism—Juvenile literature. I. Title. II. Series.
 BL1572.H37 2009
 295—dc22

                    2008035811

Chelsea House books are available at special discounts when purchased in bulk quantities for businesses, associations, institutions, or sales promotions. Please call our Special Sales Department in New York at (212) 967-8800 or (800) 322-8755.

You can find Chelsea House on the World Wide Web at http://www.chelseahouse.com

This book was produced for Chelsea House by Bender Richardson White, Uxbridge, U.K.
Project Editor: Lionel Bender
Text Editor: Ronne Randall
Designer: Ben White
Picture Researchers: Joanne O'Brien and Kim Richardson
Maps and symbols: Stefan Chabluk

Printed in China

CP BRW 10 9 8 7 6 5 4 3 2 1

This book is printed on acid-free paper.

All links and Web addresses were checked and verified to be correct at the time of publication. Because of the dynamic nature of the Web, some addresses and links may have changed since publication and may no longer be valid.

CONTENTS

PREFACE

Almost from the start of civilization, more than 10,000 years ago, religion has shaped human history. Today more than half the world's population practice a major religion or indigenous spiritual tradition. In many 21st-century societies, including the United States, religion still shapes people's lives and plays a key role in politics and culture. And in societies throughout the world increasing ethnic and cultural diversity has led to a variety of religions being practiced side by side. This makes it vital that we understand as much as we can about the world's religions.

The World Religions series, of which this book is a part, sets out to achieve this aim. It is written and designed to appeal to both students and general readers. The books offer clear, accessible overviews of the major religious traditions and institutions of our time. Each volume in the series describes where a particular religion is practiced, its origins and history, its central beliefs and important rituals, and its contributions to world civilization. Carefully chosen photographs complement the text, and sidebars, a map, fact file, glossary, bibliography, and index are included to help readers gain a more complete understanding of the subject at hand.

These books will help clarify what religion is all about and reveal both the similarities and differences in the great spiritual traditions practiced around the world today.

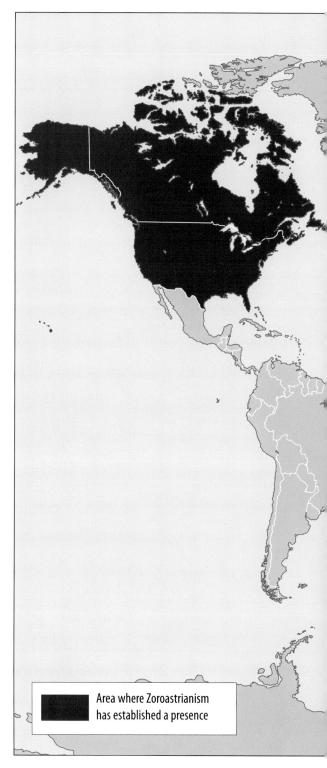

■ Area where Zoroastrianism has established a presence

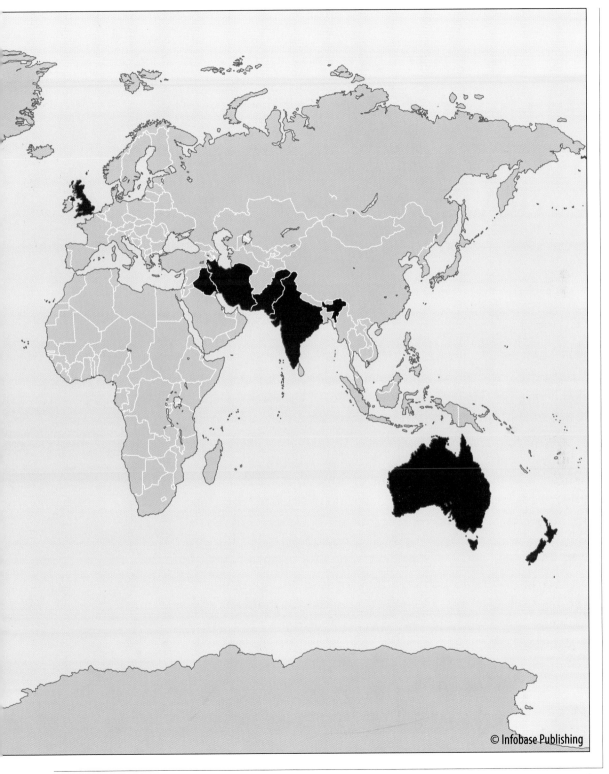

CHAPTER 1

INTRODUCTION: THE GOOD RELIGION OF ZARATHUSTRA

Zoroastrianism is one of the oldest world religions—it arose in ancient Persia (present-day Iran) around 3,500 years ago. At that time the prophet Zarathustra—Zoroaster, as the Greeks called him—began preaching his message. Zarathustra, thought to be a priest of the existing Iranian religion of his time, was a highly original thinker and a bold reformer. His teachings may seem straightforward today, but in his time they were truly revolutionary.

Zarathustra rejected many of the beliefs and practices of the existing religion. In a time of many gods he preached about one great and supreme God, Ahura Mazda. In a time when most people believed that worship consisted mainly of elaborate rituals to satisfy angry deities, he preached a religion of personal ethics in which people's actions in life were more important than ritual and sacrifice. Zarathustra's preaching formed the basis of one of the most influential and long-lasting religions the world has ever known. His message is preserved in the Avesta, the Zoroastrian scripture.

A Zoroastrian priest inside a fire temple in Isfahan, Iran. The fire room, where the sacred fire continually burns, is at the center of the building.

Zoroastrianism is the smallest of today's world religions. There are an estimated 200,000 followers. This is a tiny minority compared with world religions such as Christianity and Islam, both of which have more than one billion followers. Yet Zoroastrians or, as many of them prefer to be called, *Zarathushtis,* are a proud and active group working hard to keep their religion alive and strong.

Zoroastrians are scattered all over the world. In Iran, the land where Zoroastrianism was born, only a small number of Zoroastrians remain. There are today about 30,000 Iranian Zoroastrians, or *Zartoshtis.* The largest concentration of Zoroastrians by far, about 70,000, live in India, where they are known as *Parsis,* a name that reflects their Persian heritage. Another 5,000 live in India's neighbor Pakistan.

Zoroastrians have established themselves in many countries. There are formally organized Zoroastrian federations in Australia and New Zealand, in England, in Singapore, in Germany, and in Scandinavia among other places. North America has 20,000 Zoroastrian followers who belong to Zoroastrian organizations—in Boston, New York, Chicago, Houston, California, Washington State, Arizona, and Toronto. In the rest of the world, mainly Dubai, Australia, New Zealand, Hong Kong and Singapore, there are a further 30,000.

THE BASIC PRINCIPLES OF ZOROASTRIANISM

Zarathustra revealed his vision of the good religion in a series of psalms, or *Gathas.* The Gathas are personal expressions of Zarathustra's belief in the supreme God Ahura Mazda and conversations with him. There are many other scriptures such as the Yasna, the liturgy of sacrifice; the *Visperad,* a minor liturgical text that contains praises to Zoroaster and other spiritual leaders, the *Videvdad,* (also called the *Videvdat*), which contains the

Spiritual progress

Zoroastrian religion is defined in the Avesta scriptures as *daenaam vanghuhim,* "the good religion." It is often referred to by this title because of its emphasis on righteous thought and behavior.

THE LORD'S PRAYER

The *faravahar* or *farohar* is the symbol of Zoroastrianism. It reminds people of the purpose of their lives on earth, which is spiritual progress. The symbol is very ancient; the *fravashi* symbol decorated the walls of Persepolis more than 2,500 years ago. It represents the link between the spiritual and physical worlds.

The human form in the center is encircled by a ring that represents the eternal soul. The figure's head reminds people that they have free will, a mind and an intellect with which to choose good. The right hand points upward to lead people toward Asha, the path of Truth. In the left hand is a ring symbolizing the just power of Khshathra Vairya.

The figure has wings to help the soul fly upward and progress. It has a tail that serves as a rudder to help the soul balance between the opposing forces of good and evil. These forces are represented by the curved hooks on either side of the tail. The three sections of the tail, which appear as layers of feathers, remind people of good thoughts, good words, and good deeds.

Throughout life the human soul is caught between good and evil, Truth and The Lie. However with the heavenly help, or wings, of Ahura Mazda, the soul may soar to eternal goodness and light.

A relief sculpture of the Zoroastrian symbol, the *faravahar*, decorates a wall in the ruins of Persepolis.

Zoroastrian creation story as well as the framework of Zoroastrian law; the *Yashts* or hymns to angels and heroes; and the *Khurda* (or *Khorda*) *Avesta* ("Little Avesta") which is essentially the Zorastrian book of common prayer. The bulk of the Zoroastrian beliefs and rituals are based on these and the Gathas.

There are three basic principles of Zoroastrianism. They are:

One God—Zarathustra preached the existence of one supreme God, whose name, Ahura Mazda, means "Wise Lord." Ahura Mazda is the creator of the universe and all things in it, including humankind. Zarathustra taught that Ahura Mazda is all-good and all-wise. He is the father of truth and goodness. He brings love and happiness and is to be loved and respected, never feared.

The Twin Spirits: Truth and The Lie—According to Zoroastrian belief Ahura Mazda first created consciousness and a knowledge of perfect good, which is the spirit of Truth, or Spenta Mainyu. He then created the material world.

According to Zoroastrian cosmogony good and evil spirits have been in existence since the very beginning of created time, even before the creation of the spiritual and material worlds. Zarathustra called the Spirit of Evil "The Lie," which later came to be called Angra Mainyu or Ahriman. The struggle between the Spirit of Truth and The Lie, which never agree, governs all human thought and activity.

Free Will—Ahura Mazda does not command every aspect of human life. At the time of creation he gave humanity the gift of free will. As Zoroastrians, men and women must think and reason for themselves. They have the freedom to choose good over evil. Free will and intellect give them the choice to do the will of Ahura Mazda—to live according to the Spirit of Truth.

THE CREED OF ZOROASTRIANISM

The goal of those who follow Zoroastrian Din—the Zoroastrian religion—is to live the truth according to the principles of Ahura Mazda. Religion, Zarathustra taught, was within the individual. Each person is called upon to live according to a simple creed:

- Good Thoughts—Humata
- Good Words—Hukhta
- Good Deeds—Huvarshta

Zoroastrianism is a happy and optimistic religion. Pessimism and despair are considered sins—they represent giving in to evil. Zoroastrians are taught to love life and to enjoy life's pleasures. They are encouraged to work hard, to strive for excellence, to marry and raise families, and to be active members of the community. Enjoying festivals and social life is part of their philosophy, as is the duty to support one another in times of trouble. Zoroastrians believe that when they fight society's ills, such as sickness, poverty, and ignorance, they are working together with Ahura Mazda toward creating a perfect world. They do not practice self-denial and asceticism—that is, suffering for the sake of religious purity. In Zoroastrianism to withdraw from the world is considered sinful. Instead Zoroastrians live fully in the world, enjoying all the good things in their earthly life.

THE AMESHA SPENTAS

In the battle between the Spirit of Truth and The Lie, Ahura Mazda is assisted by the Amesha Spentas, or Benevolent Spirits, which are aspects of his own power. The Amesha Spentas are sometimes repre-

Good Thoughts

The most important goal of a Zoroastrian is to have Good Thoughts. He or she attempts to imitate the Good Mind, or Vohu Mana, one of the highest attributes of Ahura Mazda. If a person has the good mind of Zoroastrianism, he or she will speak and do good, live well, and spread happiness in the world.

sented as angelic beings, but in the spiritual sense they are sparks of the divine that every person may cultivate within himself or herself. Zoroastrians believe the highest ideal for humankind is to live these ideals.

Ahura Mazda is all-powerful, but he does not control human actions. When he gave people free will he made them responsible for their own lives and behavior. To take away free will after once giving it would be wrong. Free will and intellect offer humans the choice to do the will of Ahura Mazda—to live according to the Spirit of Truth.

THE AMESHA SPENTAS (BENEVOLENT SPIRITS)

Vohu Mana, the spirit of the Good Mind. From the Good Mind comes Good Thoughts, and from Good Thoughts follow Good Words and Good Deeds. To live according to Zoroastrianism people must strive constantly to cultivate the Good Mind within themselves, enabling them to grasp Asha. It is Vohu Mana that enables people to recognize good and evil in their lives.

Asha Vahista, the spirit of Righteousness. Asha (pronounced ah SHAH) embodies righteousness, truth, wisdom, justice, and progress. The path of Asha leads to salvation and blessing. To follow it is the highest ideal of Zoroastrianism—being righteous.

Khshathra Vairya, the spirit of Ideal Authority or Dominion. This spirit is the power of Ahura Mazda as a wise ruler. The spirit of strength and authority comes in this life to those who have the Good Mind and follow the path of Asha. In this spirit humans promote good and fight evil in the world.

Spenta Armaity, the spirit of Love and Benevolence. It is Armaity that motivates people to love humankind. Through Spenta Armaity come charity and grace.

Haurvatat, the spirit of Perfection and Well-being in this life.

Ameratat, the spirit of Immortality and Eternal Bliss.

THE *FRAVASHIS*

To help people choose the truth, each person is born with a *fravashi,* a guardian spirit that helps him or her tell good from evil, right from wrong. People may recognize their own *fravashi* when it guides their conscience. It is more than conscience, however, because a conscience must be developed as a person grows. The *fravashi* is different because it is inborn. *Fravashis* are spiritual beings that existed before the physical world was created. They are born into this world with each new life and remain with an individual until death. Then they leave to return to the company of other *fravashis,* remaining, however, a link between the living and the dead. They may be ritually called upon to communicate with the soul of the dead person. The *fravashi* is the spark of the divine essence of Ahura Mazda that is in all living things.

THE RESTORATION OF THE WORLD

Zoroastrians believe that the battle between Ahura Mazda, the perfect good, and Angra Mainyu, the evil spirit, will continue to rage unabated for several thousands of years hence. At the end of this period a savior, or *sashoyant,* will lead people successfully and definitively against the forces of evil and ignorance. There will be a mighty battle between Ahura Mazda and Angra Mainyu. The world will be overcome and destroyed by fire. Molten metal will cover the earth like water. The righteous will wade through but the unrighteous will be consumed by it. Evil, sin, and death will be defeated. The world will be purified and perfected.

In the renewal of the world all the dead will rise. The gates of hell will open and those souls too will rise, purified and redeemed. People will live together in harmony in the perfect world of Ahura Maz-

FROM THE GATHAS OF ZARATHUSTRA

In the Gathas, Zarathustra revealed his vision of the good religion in a series of psalms. There are 17 psalms composed in total. This is one of them.

When, at the time of awarding, men, with the help of Truth, shall vanquish the lie;

When deception and untruth— for long decried—of false gods and men, stand exposed,

Then, at the time of salvation, there shall be full adoration of Thy Glory.

—Ys. 48.1

da for all eternity. This time it is called frashogard, or *frashokereti,* which means "renewal."

All Zoroastrians have a duty to fight constantly against the weaknesses within the human heart and the worldly temptations that form The Lie. The forces of good, which Ahura Mazda leads, are engaged in a continual struggle with the forces of evil. In choosing good Zoroastrians join with Ahura Mazda to help bring about a perfect world.

Zoroastrian priests from the Parsi community in Mumbai, India. The Zoroastrian religion arose in ancient Persia through the preaching and teaching of the prophet Zarathustra. Around the 10th century, under increasing persecution, the first group of Zoroastrians left Persia and settled in India.

THE IMPORTANCE OF DOING GOOD

Zarathustra urged his followers to care for and defend the poor. Since the very beginning of the religion service to others has been a principle of Zoroastrianism. Every Zoroastrian is expected to share happiness, which means sharing wealth, time, and talents freely and generously. For Zoroastrians it is not enough just to think good thoughts and speak good words—one must actively work to combat evil and ignorance. In everything they do they are asked to consider not only their own welfare, but the welfare of the community. This is the spirit of Armaity, which encourages people to reach out to others in goodness and charity.

Zoroastrians are known for supporting each other in spiritual and practical ways. However they also contribute to worthy causes outside the Zoroastrian community. In India, where Zoroastrians have had a long presence, many schools, hospitals, and other worthwhile projects for use by people of whatever religion or background were founded with Zoroastrian time, energy, and financial assistance. In actively serving their communities Zoroastrians are following their Prophet and living their religion.

ZOROASTRIAN WORSHIP

Zoroastrianism is not a congregational religion. It has rich and meaningful rituals, which priests perform on a regular daily basis in their largest and most sacred places of worship, but laypeople are not expected to attend. Zoroastrians gather mainly for the New Year, or Navruz, festival and the six major festivals, or *gahambars,* which occur throughout the year. On these occasions they get together for prayers followed by a shared meal and cultural activities such as singing and dancing.

THE SACRED FIRE

For Zoroastrians fire is the sacred symbol of Ahura Mazda. It captures the brilliance of the sun and the heavenly bodies, and

Gahs

Prayers are said individually or in family groups. The day is divided into five ritual periods, or *gahs.* They occur in the morning, midday, afternoon, evening, and at night. At each of these times a Zoroastrian pauses to repeat the appropriate prayer from the Avesta, the Zoroastrian scripture.

it speaks of the power, might, and energy of the Spirit of Truth. In its purest form it represents the highest truth. Priests conduct all religious rituals and ceremonies in the presence of fire, which signifies the presence of Ahura Mazda. The most sacred fires of Zoroastrianism are consecrated fires, which contain fire from 16 different sources ritually combined in a long series of purification rites. One part of a consecrated fire is fire caused by lightning, since it comes directly from Ahura Mazda.

It is important to remember, however, that Zoroastrians do not worship fire. The sacred fire is not an object of worship in itself but a symbol and reminder of Ahura Mazda, the Wise Lord and great God.

SACRED PLACES: FIRE TEMPLES

Inside the fire temple is an entrance hall with a source of water so that people may bathe the exposed parts of their bodies before prayer. Like fire, water is a sacred creation of Ahura Mazda, and people offer prayers before it as well. At the center of the building is the "fire room." This room contains the *afargan*, a large urn that holds the fire. The fire is kept burning day and night. It is tended regularly by priests in a ceremony known as *boi*. The fire room has no decorations. There are no statues and no pictures on the wall—nothing to detract from the beauty and power of the fire.

In the rest of the fire temple are meeting rooms, lecture halls, and a library. These rooms, which have no sacred significance, may have portraits or plaques commemorating donors and paintings that represent the prophet Zarathustra. The entrances to the building are often decorated with flowers and beadwork, signifying that the building is a place of tranquility, purity, and happiness.

ATASH BEHRAM

In an *atash behram* only fully initiated priests may enter the fire room. Properly initiated and ritually pure Zoroastrian worshippers may, if they wish, observe the rites through iron bars or grillwork that separate them from the sacred fire.

The ruins of an ancient Zoroastrian fire temple stand on a
hill near Isfahan, Iran. The dramatic setting suggests the
importance placed on worship.

FIRE TEMPLES

Fire temples house the sacred fires of Zoroastrianism. There are three grades of fire temple: *atash behram, atash adaran,* and *atash dadgah*. An *atash behram* is the highest grade of temple. Sometimes referred to as a "fire cathedral," it houses the holiest of consecrated fires. The highest and most sacred of all Zoroastrian rituals are held there, conducted by the high priests of Zoroastrianism. There are only 10 *atash behrams* in the world: eight in India and two in Iran.

A priest, or *mobed,* attending a consecrated fire in a temple in Isfahan, Iran.

ATASH ADARAN

An *atash adaran* also houses consecrated fire. It differs from an *atash behram* in the number of rituals performed in establishing the temple and the number and type of ceremonies a priest must perform before entering the fire room.

ATASH DADGA

The fire in an *atash dadga* is similar to a household fire. Although still worthy of reverence, it is not specially consecrated. In India this grade of temple is known as an *agiary*. In North America it is called a *darbe mehr* or *dar-e meher*. No high rituals are held there and there may be no full-time priest. If the fire is kept burning at all times it may be fed by a layperson who has bathed and put on clean clothes. Special ceremonies such as weddings, funerals, and initiations are performed by priests who come for the occasion. These too are always performed in the presence of fire.

ZOROASTRIANISM AND OTHER RELIGIONS

Zoroastrianism has much in common with other world religions, several of which it influenced. Like religions such as Judaism, Christianity, and Islam it is monotheistic—that is, its followers believe in one supreme God. They believe in life after death and in heaven and hell. Zoroastrianism also has a strong code of ethics that its believers are expected to follow in their daily lives. Like Christianity, Islam, and Buddhism it had a specific founder who came to reform older religious practices. However it differs from other religions in significant ways. Unlike Islam it is not fatalistic. The evil in the world is not the will of God but exists because of flaws in the material world and within the human heart. Zoroastrians control their destiny after death by their actions on earth, their choice of good and truth over ignorance and evil.

Like Christians and Jews, Zoroastrians believe that a savior will come at the end of time to lead the faithful into a perfected world. However Zoroastrianism differs from Christianity, whose believers are saved by faith in Jesus Christ and by God's grace rather than by their good works. Also, Zoroastrians do not believe in original sin. People are born pure but may be influenced by the evil around them. For Zoroastrians it is a lifetime of following the teachings of Zarathustra that brings about salvation, not faith alone. Zoroastrianism also differs from Hinduism in that there is no belief in reincarnation and no transmigration of the soul. People live on this earth but once and have only one chance to find their way to eternal peace.

THE IMPORTANCE OF ZOROASTRIANISM

The remains of the palace at Pasargardae, Iran. This is the capital established by the emperor Cyrus, who ascended to the Persian throne in 559 B.C.E. During his reign he continued to expand his empire as far as the shores of the Aegean. Cyrus may have been a follower of Zoroastrianism but this is not certain.

Zoroastrianism holds a unique place in the history of religion. Its founder and prophet, Zarathustra, originated the concept of one great and supreme God. He proposed an explanation for the problem of evil in a world created by a good God through the notion of the twin mentalities, the Spirit of Truth and The Lie, which are present in the human heart, and through the imperfection in the material world. Zoroastrianism thus answers the question with which all religions must struggle: "How can a good and loving God permit evil and suffering in the world?" Zoroastrians believe that evil and suffering are the work of the Lie,

Angra Mainyu, and not of Ahura Mazda, who battles evil and sin and will eventually defeat it.

AFTERLIFE AND FINAL JUDGMENT

Zarathustra also introduced the concept of an afterlife in which people would be welcomed into the glory of Ahura Mazda or dropped into the pit—representing hell—as a result of their actions on earth. In Angra Mainyu, Zoroastrianism gave the world the concept of Satan, the tempter and ruler of the underworld.

Zarathustra spoke of a savior who would come to lead the righteous at the end of the world, and of a final judgment in which the existing world would be destroyed and a new, perfect world would come into being. He offered humankind free will with which to choose good over evil in order to perfect the world in a joint venture with Ahura Mazda. He changed the ancient Iranian polytheistic (the belief in more than one god) notion of religion as a way of attempting to calm angry gods to one of ethical actions on the part of humans. In the ancient Iranian society where women had lesser roles to play, he declared that they were religiously equal to men and also capable of salvation.

INFLUENCE OF ZOROASTRIANISM

Zoroastrianism is believed to have influenced other world religions with which it came into contact. Some see Cyrus, the great king of Persia who liberated the Jews in 537 B.C.E. from their captivity in the ancient city of Babylon (near present-day Baghdad, Iraq), as one who brought the Zoroastrian monotheistic view of God to the Hebrew people and through them to Christianity. Zoroastrian teachings such as heaven and hell and final judgment also are viewed as having entered Islam when Muslim rulers took over Persia in the seventh century C.E.

Most of all Zoroastrianism has proved to be a durable and lasting faith. Its followers, although few in number, are the proud keepers of a heritage that goes back thousands of years.

CHAPTER 2

ZARATHUSTRA, FATHER OF ZOROASTRIANISM

Few facts can be known about Zarathustra, or Zoroaster, as the Greeks called him. It is known that he was a real person and that he lived in very ancient times. During his lifetime the peoples of the Iranian Plateau, his homeland, kept no written documents, so there are no eyewitness accounts of his life. It is not even known for certain when he lived. The Greeks, who wrote of him first, knew only that the traditions concerning his life were already centuries old. They estimated that he had lived some 6,000 years earlier than the philosopher Plato (ca. 429–ca. 347 B.C.E.). Later historians reckoned that Zarathustra had lived around 600 B.C.E., around the time of the Hebrew prophets. Today's scholars believe that Zarathustra lived between 1500 and 1000 B.C.E. However even this is a wide range of time.

The earliest versions of Zarathustra's life were passed down orally (by mouth) for more than a thousand years before they were recorded in writing, so it is hard to know how accurate they are. However, they provide some important clues to the man and his life. Knowledge of Zarathustra comes from his own writings and his influence. One way scholars trace Zarathustra's life

A shrine to Zarathustra in a Parsi home in Karachi, Pakistan, includes representation of the prophet and a continuously burning fire.

is by looking for clues in the Gathas, the ancient hymns that are believed to have been the work of Zarathustra himself.

ZARATHUSTRA'S WORDS

Throughout his life Zarathustra composed hymns or psalms to the glory of Ahura Mazda. They are composed in Zarathustra's language, Gathic Avestan. The Gathas are poems in complex metrical forms that were difficult to master. In Zarathustra's time such learning was largely confined to the priesthood, and his use of poetic form suggests that he had priestly training. The Gathas are of high literary quality. They show Zarathustra to have been not only a great religious thinker, but also one of Persia's earliest and finest poets.

ZARATHUSTRA'S PROBABLE ORIGINS

Although many areas of Iran have claimed him, Zarathustra was probably born in what was then northeastern Persia, roughly where the boundaries of modern Iran, Afghanistan, and Turkmenistan meet today. Persia—which eventually stretched from the prairieland of Russia and the Caspian Sea westward to the Greek Empire and south toward modern Pakistan—had not yet become an empire.

From the Avesta, the Zoroastrian holy book, the names of Zarathustra's mother, Dughda, and his father, Pourushasp, of the Spitama clan are known. Tradition has it that Zarathustra was born in their home on the banks of the Daraja River. His followers celebrate his birthday on the sixth day of the first month, Farvardin (March–April) on the Zoroastrian calendar.

The Spitamas were a pastoral people who probably raised and traded horses.

Visionary Image

Gathic Avestan, the language of the Gathas, is a very ancient dialect, one that was spoken only in a small area and for a relatively short time. This dialect provides important clues to Zarathustra's origins.

Since he lived more than 3,000 years ago, no one knows what Zarathustra looked like. Artistic renderings of him, however, all look alike, even to the pose—a man gazing upward to the right, one hand raised. Until the 18th century there were no portraits of Zarathustra. Then a Zoroastrian artist had a dream in which the Prophet appeared to him. He painted the man he saw and Zoroastrians since that time have accepted his vision as the way Zarathustra looked.

A portrait of Zarathustra.

Zarathustra himself, however, was apparently drawn to religion from an early age. The Gathas he composed suggest that he knew the religious traditions well and had been trained as a priest.

ZARATHUSTRA'S MIRACULOUS BEGINNINGS

According to the later legendary Zoroastrian tradition, the coming of Zarathustra was foretold long before his birth. The creatures of the earth and the saints of the heavens had spoken of it from the beginnings of the world. The heavenly glory that would pass to Zarathustra came from the sun, moon, and stars into the home of Zarathustra's mother, Dughda, even before her birth, starting an ever-burning fire on the hearth. When Dughda was born, she glowed with light. Evil powers tried to convince Dughda's father that the light around her showed she was a sorceress.

Flames from a fire.
Consecrated fire is central to
Zoroastrian rituals.

He sent her away from his home, but in her new home she met Pourushasp, who was to be her husband.

HAOMA—THE SACRED PLANT

As Dughda and Pourushasp were walking Dughda saw and admired a plant. Pourushasp picked it for her and carried it home. It was a *haoma*, the sacred plant of Zoroastrian ritual. Inside was hidden Zarathustra's guardian spirit, or *fravahi*, which would join him at birth. In this way the divine spirit came into their home. Zarathustra was born soon afterward, surrounded by light. As a newborn baby he laughed and he spoke to Ahura Mazda, dedicating his life to the Wise Lord.

PROTECTING ANIMALS

Zoroastrian legend says that evil spirits set out immediately to destroy this child that would conquer them. They persuaded the evil local chieftain that the radiant infant was a demon. The chieftain laid the child on a pile of firewood and tried to light it, but the fire would not burn. Then he put the baby in the path of stampeding oxen, but the first ox stood over the baby and protected him. Zarathustra was put into the den of a wolf whose cubs had been taken away, but instead of harming him the wolf cared for him.

The theme of Zarathustra's special relationship with animals recurs, underscoring his protection of them from animal sacrifice. Zarathustra survived other trials as a baby and child, always protected by his own essential goodness and righteousness.

Zarathustra's Birth

The miraculous happenings surrounding Zarathustra's birth tie elements of Zoroastrianism, such as the sacred fire and the *haoma* plant, to the life of the Prophet. These traditions glorify the life of a man of humble origins whose thought and philosophy were a turning point in religious history.

The Birth of Zarathustra, from the *Denkard* portion of the Avesta:

Further, when he [Zarathustra] was born, there was a light like the blaze of fire, a glare and a twilight irradiating from his house in all directions, high in the air and to a great distance on the earth, as a token of his greatness and exaltation . . .

(In *Denkard*, Book 5, Chapter 2, edited by Peshotun Dastoor Behramjee Sanjana.)

THE ZOROASTRIAN TRADITION

The Greeks first learned of Zoroaster and his message around 400 B.C.E. from the Magi, a priestly tribe of western Iran. By then Zoroastrianism had had time to spread from the extreme eastern boundaries of Iran to the west. The Magi adopted Zoroastrian belief and claimed Zarathustra as one of their own. They placed him as having lived some 200 years earlier. The writings written in Pahlavi, the language of Avesta commentary, gave the date of his birth as somewhere between 630 and 618 B.C.E., about a hundred years before the time of the Persian ruler Cyrus the Great.

When Zarathustra was 15, according to the local custom he was considered an adult. He put on the sacred sash of the existing Iranian religion and took up adult duties. However he was restless. Born into violent times, he had seen much human suffering. Even at this young age he had begun to consider the question of righteousness and the conflict between good and evil in the world. At the age of 20, over his parents' objections, he left home and began a period of wandering inquiring about the nature of righteousness.

ZARATHUSTRA'S EARLY MINISTRY

From the age of 20 to the age of 30 Zarathustra lived in solitude on a mountain, searching for answers. At the age of 30, in order to participate as a member of a priestly family in the spring festival, he went to the famous Daitya River, where

The landscape of Iran. Zarathustra undertook a period of wandering through this land to further understand questions regarding the nature of good and evil.

Zarathustra tells of his vision of Ahura Mazda in the Gathas:

Then thus spake Ahura Mazda, the Lord of knowledge and wisdom:

"As there is not a righteous spiritual lord, or secular chief

So have I, indeed, the Creator, made thee, Zarathustra, the leader,

For the welfare of the world and its diligent people."

—Ys. 29.6

Scarcely able to believe what he hears, Zarathustra asks whom Ahura Mazda has chosen to carry his divine word and the welfare of the world. Ahura Mazda responds:

And thus spoke Ahura Mazda: "The one who alone has harkened to my command and is known to me is Zarathustra Spitama.

For his creator and for Truth, he wishes to announce the Holy Message,

Wherefore shall I bestow on him, the charm of speech."

—Ys. 29.8

In this way Zarathustra is ordained to be Ahura Mazda's prophet and receives directly from him the gift of preaching.

one of his priestly duties was to go to the river at dawn to draw water from the deepest and purest part of the stream for the morning ceremony. As he waded back to the riverbank a glorious angel, Vohu Mana, stood before him. The angel asked him who he was and what was the most important thing in his life. Zarathustra replied that he wanted most of all to be righteous and pure and to gain wisdom. With that the angel took Zarathustra into the presence of Ahura Mazda and the archangels.

Zarathustra understood that he had received a special calling. He also understood that the way would be difficult because it meant opposing the old religion and the princes who used it to their own ends. During the next few years he often felt despair and called on Ahura Mazda to help him. He received other visions, seven in all, in which one by one all of the archangels, or Beneficent Immortals, appeared to him. These visions helped him to remain faithful to his work. From the age of 30, when he received his revelation, to the age of 42, when he was accepted as a prophet by Vishtaspa, the king of Bactria, Zarathustra wandered from place to place, from the west to the east of Iran.

ZARATHUSTRA'S MESSAGE

Zarathustra arose as a prophet who strongly denounced the ritual practices of the warrior societies, the groups of young men who wandered the countryside in a state of drunkenness, stealing and slaughtering cattle and terrorizing people. An outspoken reformer, Zarathustra fought against the cruel and bloody practice of animal sacrifice, the use of intoxicating herbs, and the excesses of the old religion that whipped young men into a frenzy and sent them into battle. Never afraid to speak out, he openly scorned the "mumbling" priests and sacrificers. Instead of ritual he demanded that people turn their hearts and minds to Ahura Mazda.

Zarathustra preached the notion of one true god, Ahura Mazda, who had created human life and all things visible and invisible. Along with all the things of the earth, two opposing forces were created. One force, Spenta Mainyu, the holy spirit, represented Truth and Goodness. The other, a destructive spirit that came to be called Angra Mainyu, represented the Lie. Zarathustra saw a world of ethical good in which people worked to maintain life by marrying, bringing up children, raising cattle, and farming. They would think good thoughts and do good deeds, turning away from evil and creating a peaceful, loving society. After death people would be judged according to how they had chosen to live their lives. It was up to humans to choose Truth over The Lie. He also taught that the world would end and that at that time the righteous would be saved and the evildoers would go down into the underworld.

ZARATHUSTRA WINS CONVERTS

For the first 10 years of his mission Zarathustra traveled around preaching in the

Yatha Ahu Vairyo

One of the greatest Zoroastrian prayers, believed to have been composed by Zarathustra, this prayer is spoken by the priest in confirmation, wedding, and funeral ceremonies.

Yatha ahu vairyo, atha ratush ashatcit haca, vangheush dazda manangho, shyaothananam angheush mazdai, xshathremca ahurai a, yim drigubyo dadat vastarem.

The gift of the good mind leads to actions dedicated to Ahura Mazda. Ahura Mazda gives authority to the one who protects the dispossessed.

Revolutionary Ideas

The ideas of one supreme God, the struggle between good and evil in the human soul, and a last judgment after death do not seem very unusual today, but in Zarathustra's time they were revolutionary. Also revolutionary was his declaration that women, who held little or no place in society, were equal with men in the sight of Ahura Mazda and had the same hope of salvation.

Head of the *faravahar* symbol in the entrance to a Zoroastrian temple in Iran. The head reminds people that they have free will, a mind, and an intellect with which to choose right.

courts of local rulers. His efforts were unsuccessful. At the age of 40, after 10 years of preaching and teaching, Zarathustra finally made his first convert. It was his cousin Maidyoimanha (also known asor Medyomah), the son of his father's brother. This was an important milestone but Zarathustra himself wondered whether the struggle was worthwhile—in 10 years he had won only one person to the side of Ahura Mazda.

ZARATHUSTRA FLEES

Meanwhile Zarathustra's preaching had caused him many problems. He had angered the priests and teachers of the existing order. They denounced him and his message.

Zarathustra fled and took refuge in the court of Kai Vishtaspa, King of the ancient city of Bactra (what is now northern Afghanistan). At first he was not well received; for a time he languished in prison. As the story goes Vishtaspa had a favorite horse that had become paralyzed, its legs drawn up into its body. Zarathustra restored the horse to health and made converts of Vishtaspa, his family, and his court. One who accepted Zarathustra's preaching from the start was Jamaspa, the kingdom's prime minister, who was to become Zarathustra's spiritual successor. By this time Zarathustra was 42 years old.

FIGHTING FOR BELIEFS

The conversion of Vishtaspa proved to be a turning point. With the king's support and patronage Zarathustra was free to preach and spread his message, but even then things did not go smoothly. Rulers of the surrounding kingdoms attacked Vishtaspa in an attempt to get him to renounce Zarathustra's way. Fortunately for Zarathustra and for Zoroastrianism, Vishtaspa and his sons were willing to fight for what they believed. Vishtaspa was forced to fight two wars in defense of

Finding Solace

After being denounced by priests and teachers of the existing order Zarathustra turned in despair to Ahura Mazda:

To what land shall I flee? Where bend my steps?
I am thrust out from family and tribe:
I have no favor from the village to which I would belong,
Nor from the wicked rulers of the country.

—Ushtavaiti Gatha, Ys. 46.1

Zoroastrianism. Vishtaspa's army proved to be a formidable fighting force. His son Prince Asfandyar defeated attackers and signed new treaties across Persia. Zarathustra's message spread.

ZARATHUSTRA'S LATER LIFE

Zarathustra preached that people should live in the real world, working, marrying, and raising families.

The Gathas (13.98, 13.9) describe the wedding of Zarathustra's youngest daughter, Pouruchista, to Jamaspa, the prime minister of Vishtaspa, as an occasion of much joy. In keeping with his belief that people should choose freely among the options in their lives, Zarathustra speaks to his daughter about Jamaspa's good qualities but allows her to choose for herself. With the marriage of Pouruchista and Jamaspa a new generation of Zoroastrians began.

THE DEATH OF ZARATHUSTRA

Zarathustra lived into old age. Zoroastrianism was spreading across the Persian landscape. However the new religion still had its detractors, particularly the priests of the old religion that Zoroastrianism was replacing. At age 77 Zarathustra was preaching in Vishtaspa's court when the place was attacked and he was killed. Some say that he was assassinated with a ritual dagger by a priest of the old order who could not bear to have Zarathustra's message spread in the world; others say that he died at the hands of the soldiers. Regardless of how he died, the Zoroastrian fire could not be quenched. By the end of his life Zarathustra's message had taken root. It was not only to spread throughout Persia, but to have a far-reaching influence on other world religions as well.

CHAPTER 3

ZOROASTRIANISM THROUGH HISTORY

Zoroastrianism began and flourished on the Iranian Plain in the land that became Persia, one of the great civilizations of the ancient world. However the history of Zoroastrianism goes back much further than the Persian Empire. By the time Persian culture reached its height, between the sixth and fourth centuries B.C.E., Zoroastrianism was already many centuries old.

Probably more than a thousand years passed between the time when Zarathustra lived and the time when any history of the land and its peoples began to be written down. Even then written history came not from the Persians, who left few written records of their own, but from the Greeks and other outside sources. Most of what is known today about the Persians and their time comes from Greek writings, from archaeological and language studies, and from the Avesta, the Zoroastrian holy book, which preserved oral history and legends.

ARYAN MIGRATIONS

Scholars believe that the people who settled the Iranian Plain migrated there between 2000 and 1500 B.C.E. from what is now

The ruins of the palace of Persepolis built by the emperor Darius and destroyed by Alexander the Great in 330 B.C.E.

southern Russia. From studying their languages it is known that they were of European, or Aryan, background rather than from the Middle East. The land the travelers found was unwelcoming—high, rugged mountains surrounded a dry salt desert. It was a land that was blisteringly hot in summer and frigid in winter. People gathered in the low valleys and along rivers, where they could farm and herd animals.

The migrants formed tribes. Mixing with the people who were already living in the areas they settled, and widely separated from other migrant groups, they developed distinct dialects, or variations of languages. The two largest tribes were the Medes in the land called Media to the north, and the Persians in the south, but there were also others. Each was made up of smaller subgroups. Many, including the group into which Zarathustra was born, apparently lived peacefully, farming and herding cattle and other livestock, the mainstay of their existence.

The migrants brought their rituals and beliefs with them from a still older time. The early Iranians practiced an ancient polytheistic religion about which little is known. However its rituals included animal sacrifice and the use of intoxicating drugs to appease angry gods. Some of these rituals also served as a way to prepare young men for battle by rousing them into a state of frenzy. These young men formed warrior societies that crossed and recrossed the plains on horseback, raiding and plundering, stealing cattle and laying waste to farmland. So although many tribes lived peacefully, the times were scarred by violence and cruelty.

EARLY ZOROASTRIANISM

The prophet Zarathustra came as a reformer to change the practices of the ancient Iranian religion. He preached against the excesses of ritual that led to drunken raiding and the senseless slaughter of cattle. His message was that people should focus their thoughts on one wise and good God, Ahura Mazda. Eventually Zoroastrianism took root in the kingdom of Bactria ruled by Kai Vishtaspa.

Vishtaspa was one of the rulers of the legendary Kayanian dynasty that ruled in Iran in prehistory. Little is known about him except that he adopted the new religion preached by Zarathustra and that he was willing to defend his belief by fighting for it. Vishtaspa's support enabled Zoroastrianism to grow.

After Zarathustra's death the leadership of the new religion passed to Zarathustra's son-in-law, Jamaspa, an official of Vishtaspa's court. Gradually the religion moved outward from Vishtaspa's kingdom into other parts of Persia. For a thousand years after Zarathustra's lifetime Zoroastrianism continued to spread across the Iranian Plain.

ZOROASTRIANISM GROWS AND CHANGES

The Zoroastrianism that developed in the centuries after Zarathustra's death changed in some ways from the Prophet's original vision. For one thing Zarathustra had preached against the excesses of the ancient rituals. Nonetheless as Zoroastrianism became more widely accepted ritual returned. No longer, however, was its purpose to appease warlike gods and whip soldiers into a frenzy for battle. The rituals of Zoroastrianism focused on praising and worshipping Ahura Mazda. Many rituals of Zoroastrianism reached back to the ancient Iranian religion that had gone before it. This is not surprising since Zarathustra had been a reformer of the old religion, not the founder of a whole new religion. While boldly new in many ways, it had retained familiar elements, and returning to the old rituals seemed a natural step for its followers.

THE MAGI

As Zoroastrianism swept westward it encountered the Magi, a priestly tribe of Medes. The Magi had long held the secrets of priestly ritual for the Median people. They were also the keepers of medical lore

HAOMA RITE

One ceremony that returned to the old rituals Zarathustra usually preached against involved the plant *haoma*. No one today is sure what plant had been used by the ancient priests. However in the new *haoma* rite, it was ritually pounded to give up its juice. Mixed with milk, it was offered to Ahura Mazda, and small quantities were used by priests to help them obtain visions seeking the path of truth. The *haoma* ritual became one of the main rites of Zoroastrianism.

A traditional Christian crib depicting the Nativity, the birth of Jesus. Christians recognize the Zoroastrian priests as the Magi, the "Three Wise Men" who followed a star to Bethlehem to see the infant Jesus.

and of the knowledge of astronomy. Sometime around the eighth century they adopted Zoroastrianism and claimed Zarathustra as one of their own. They brought additional ritual practices to the religion along with their knowledge of the stars. It was the Magi who first presented and taught the teachings of Zarathustra to the Greeks.

Over time Zoroastrianism changed in other ways as well. Zarathustra had not given bodily form to concepts of good and evil and to the Amesha Spentas. However in the following centuries these abstract ideas became more concrete. The Amesha Spentas became the Beneficent Immortals, archangels that fought alongside Ahura Mazda in the battle against evil. Evil itself was given a name—Angra Mainyu, the Lie. Now people could visualize more easily the struggle between Truth and the Lie. Other ideas became concrete too. People told of Ahura Mazda's creation of the world, and this too became part of Zoroastrian belief.

CYRUS THE GREAT AND THE ACHAEMENID EMPIRE

In 575 B.C.E. a Persian royal child, Cyrus, was born (in what is modern-day Iran). Young Cyrus showed an early talent for leadership. In 559 he ascended to the Persian throne. A powerful Median kingdom had ruled the Persians for more than a century, but its influence was waning. The Median ruler challenged the young Persian king to battle in 549 and Cyrus defeated him. Cyrus took control of Media. Eventually his armies conquered the lands from Babylonia to the south and up into central Asia to the north. His defeat of Babylon freed the Jews, in bondage there to the Babylonian king. Cyrus was widely revered by the Jewish people for his wisdom and generosity. Zoroastrianism is widely believed to have mingled with Judaism at this time, influencing the Jewish religion. This was the era of the great Hebrew prophet Isaiah, who preached of a savior yet to be born into the world, an idea that previously had been Zoroastrian alone.

It is not possible to say with certainty that Cyrus was a follower of the Zarathustrian religion, although he may have been. Except for some official decrees, no written records of his reign survive, and Zoroastrianism is not mentioned by name in the Greek trading records of the time. However Zoroastrians point to his rule of justice and truth and the fact that he never tried to convert the peoples he conquered as signs that he was following the path laid down by Zarathustra.

THE ACHAEMENIDS

The imperial line Cyrus began is called the Achaemenid Empire, after his ancestor Achaemenes. After Cyrus's death in 529 B.C.E. a century of fighting and warfare under a succession of Achaemenid rulers expanded Persian rule still further, from the Mediterranean Sea and into Africa on the west and to the Indus River on the east.

GOVERNANCE AND DIPLOMACY

The Achaemenids were not only fierce warriors. They were excellent managers, diplomatic in their approach to government, who

ACHAEMENID MONARCHS

Cyrus the Great 559–529 B.C.E.

Cambyses 529–522 B.C.E.

Smerdis 522 B.C.E.

Darius I 522–485 B.C.E.

Xerxes 485–465 B.C.E.

Artaxerxes I 465–425 B.C.E.

Darius II 425–405 B.C.E.

Artaxerxes II 405–359 B.C.E.

Artaxerxes III 359–340 B.C.E.

Darius III 340–330 B.C.E.

The gates at the ancient Persian city of Pasargadae, Iran. The
tomb of the Achaemenid emperor Cyrus is in the
ruins at Pasargadae.

administered their far-flung holdings with uncommon wisdom and foresight. Within the Persian domain was a well-developed communications system so that royal decrees could reach the farthest outposts in a matter of days. The Achaemenids traded widely within and outside their empire, particularly with the Greeks. Importantly, conquered tribes were allowed to keep their own religions and customs, a practice that helped keep the peace. For example the Magi, priests of the defeated Medes, gained favor with the Achaemenid court and became the chief priests of Zoroastrianism.

DARIUS AND THE RULE OF LAW

In 522 B.C.E. Darius I became emperor. Darius continued to emphasize military power and gained an international reputation for his rule of law. He also constructed roads and established a money system of gold coins. He built two palaces, both in ancient cities of southwest Iran. He built his winter palace at Susa and his summer palace at Persepolis, famous for its architecture and lavish beauty.

Originally all Zoroastrian worship had been held outdoors around open fires. As foreign influences entered the Iranian Plain, however, probably in the fifth century B.C.E., people had begun to construct buildings so that they could hold their rituals in private.

PERSIA UNDER ALEXANDER

After 200 years on the throne the Achaemenids were no longer as powerful as they had been. In Greece the king Alexander (356-323 B.C.E.) saw a chance to extend his empire by overcoming Persia. He attacked

Rock Inscription

From an inscription on a mountain cliff at Naqsh-i Rustam, near Persepolis, the summer palace of Darius I (521–485 B.C.E.):

A great God is Ahuramazda, who created this earth, who created yonder sky, who created man, who created happiness for man, who made Darius king . . . When Ahuramazda saw this earth turbulent then he bestowed it on me, he made me king . . . This which has been done, all that by the will of Ahuramazda I did. Ahuramazda bore me aid, until I did the work. Me may Ahuramazda protect from harm, and my royal house, and this land. This I pray of Ahuramazda, this may Ahuramazda grant me! O man, that which is the command of Ahuramazda, let this not seem hateful to you. Do not leave the right path, do not rebel!

(In Mary Boyce, *Textual Sources for the Study of Zoroastrianism*, 1984.)

Alexander in battle with the Persians led by Darius III. Alexander's invasion was a disaster for Zoroastrianism. The army destroyed fire temples and slaughtered priests. Centuries of Zoroastrian learning were lost. The Zoroastrians were no longer the ruling class with a powerful priesthood. The religion was left leaderless and in disarray.

with a huge army and finally defeated the Persians under Darius III in 330 B.C.E. Alexander was ruthless in victory. He looted and burned the palace at Persepolis, stripping gold off the walls to finance his march across Persia. Although the rest of the world calls him "Alexander the Great," to Zoroastrians he became Alexander "the accursed," a name associated with Ahriman or Angra Mainyu, the evil spirit himself.

AFTER ALEXANDER: THE SELEUCIDS

After Alexander's death in 323 B.C.E. his empire was divided. In 320 B.C.E. Persia was handed over to Seleucus I. The Seleucids put up temples to their own Greek gods and tried to encourage Greek culture in Persia but their attempts were mostly unsuccessful. The Persians were fiercely proud and their hatred of the Greeks ran deep. In name the Greeks ruled Persia, but in practice people regathered in tribes, and many small kingdoms emerged. The Greek religion never replaced Zoroastrianism, which seemed, if anything, to grow stronger.

Preoccupied with wars in Egypt and other parts of the Middle Eastern world, the Seleucids gradually lost control of the vast Iranian land. By 250 B.C.E. their influence was failing. The Parthians, an Iranian tribe to the north near the Caspian Sea, declared themselves a separate state. They raised an army and defended themselves successfully against Seleucid attempts to subdue them.

PARTHIAN RULE

The Parthian ruler Mithridates I gradually gained control over all the Seleucid holdings in Persia during the second century B.C.E.. His son Mithridates II extended his rule into India to the east and as far as Syria to the south and west.

The Parthians considered themselves the heirs of the Achaemenids. Like the Achaemenids they practiced Zoroastrianism. They reconstructed fire temples that were destroyed by Alexander. In the oil-rich ground of the north, fire often occurred naturally, springing as if miraculously from the ground. The Parthian priests declared such places sacred and held fire rituals there.

Greek influence waned. By now Zoroastrianism, already well over 1,000 years old, was well established all across Persia among the ordinary people as well as in the ruling establishment.

RELIGIOUS DIVERSITY AND TOLERANCE

Parthian Persia was tolerant of religions and home to many faiths. Hindus, Buddhists, Greeks, Jews, Christians, and pagans mixed there. Under the Parthians Zoroastrianism itself had great variety. In a huge country with little communication, many ways of practicing the religion had developed. Some people worshipped Ahura Mazda in fire temples, others turned back to Mithra, an ancient god who became one of the archangels of Zoroastrian belief. Some temples had statues of Anahita, a female deity. The Parthian kings themselves followed a form of the religion that had grown up in the east, but they did not try to impose their beliefs on the people. Instead they were tolerant of all forms of worship.

GATHERING WRITTEN SOURCES

In the first century C.E. the Parthian rulers began collecting the Avestan materials that had been scattered during Alexander's invasion and writing them down. Some materials, like the Gathas, had survived more or less intact. Others were in bits and pieces, fragments of different rituals and beliefs. The Parthians set about gathering everything they could find.

Centuries of warfare with the Romans weakened the Parthians, who were overrun by Roman armies for more than 80 years before they finally gave way in 198 C.E. The Parthian royal line continued, but with little power. On the whole, however, Parthian rule had helped to strengthen Zoroastrianism.

THE SASSANIANS

As the Parthians declined another Persian empire was on the rise. This one was ruled by Ardashir, the grandson of the Persian noble Sassan. Ardashir also claimed to be descended from the Achaemenids. He defeated the last of the Parthian kings in 224 C.E. and consolidated his power over what had been their territory. Once he had brought all the Iranian kings and subkings under his control, Ardashir took on Rome. Shapur I, Ardashir's son, continued his work, defeating the Roman emperor Valerian in 259.

In matters of religion in general and Zoroastrianism in particular, the Sassanians thought the Parthians had been too liberal. To discourage the bubbling mix of religions on their soil, they made Zoroastrianism the official state religion. Then they set about standardizing it. Under the Parthians followers of different priestly traditions had developed varying forms of ritual and belief. The Sassanians decided that there should be only one. They created a national priesthood to examine the materials the Parthians had collected and to do away with any ritual forms they felt were not "pure." Through this priestly editing a standardized form of Zoroastrianism appeared. Some variety and vigor were necessarily lost, and the religion became more concerned with ritual than it had previously been, but now it was clear what was and was not Zoroastrian.

GATHERING THE AVESTA

The Sassanians continued the work of collecting and writing down the Avestan literature. They developed a special script in which to record the Gathic Avestan dialect spoken by Zarathustra as well as Zoroastrian texts in the later but still very ancient "Young Avestan," dialect, both of which had been preserved exactly in Zoroastrianism's long oral tradition.

The Sassanians also recorded other traditions of Zoroastrianism, such as the creation of the world and humankind, and they added commentaries, or *Zand,* to the growing body of literature that was the Avesta.

Pahlavi

Until the time of the Sassanians, the written language of Zoroastrianism had been Avestan. The spoken language, however, had been changing and developing. The language the Persian people spoke was what is called Pahlavi, or Middle Persian. The name of Ahura Mazda, for example, became Ohrmazd, and Angra Mainyu, the evil spirit, became Ahriman. Sassasian scribes not only copied down the ancient Gathic texts, but they translated them into the language spoken by the masses so that Pahlavi speakers could understand them without special knowledge.

ZOROASTRIANISM IN THE LATER SASSANIAN PERIOD

As the official state religion Zoroastrianism occupied a special place in Sassanian Persia. However by now Zoroastrianism had to compete with other religions that had made their way into Persia. Although these faiths were officially banned, the rigid, state-sponsored form of Zoroastrianism caused some people to turn to other beliefs. A new prophet, a young man named Mani (216–276), caught the ear of one of the Sassanian rulers. Mani's religion, called Manichaeism, was a blend of Zoroastrian, Christian, Buddhist, and Gnostic beliefs (Gnosticism was an offshoot of early Christianity). When the next ruler came into power, though, Mani fell into disfavor. He was imprisoned and later put to death. Without its leader Manichaeism's influence faded. In the fifth century, another sect, with communistic overtones, arose under a religious leader named Mazdak, but this too was put down. Although Christianity continued to spread in the west, Zoroastrianism in its Sassanian form remained the religion of the Persian people and their kings.

In 637 c.e. the Arabs attacked Persia and overwhelmed the Sassanian army. Sassanian kings remained on the throne until 651. The last of the Sassanian rulers, a young king named Yazdegard III, had taken over an empire in turmoil in 632. Ten rulers had preceded him in the previous five years, as the Arab threat grew. Yazdegard tried to fight but as Arab victories multiplied, his situation became increasingly hopeless. He turned for help to the governor of Merv, a city in southern Turkmenistan, but the governor betrayed him to the Arab forces. He was tracked down and murdered at the age of 34 in 651. The 400-year reign of the Sassanians came to an end. Muslim rulers took over Persia.

HISTORICAL PERIODS

Achaemenid Empire 550 B.C.E.–330 B.C.E.
Seleucid Empire 330 B.C.E.–250 B.C.E.
Parthian Dynasty 250 B.C.E.–226 C.E.
Sassanian Dynasty 226 C.E.–651 C.E.

ZOROASTRIANISM UNDER MUSLIM RULE

Islam swept the country along with the Muslim rulers. Many people converted voluntarily, recognizing in Islam familiar concepts of Zoroastrianism such as heaven and hell, a final judgment, and prayer

An Iranian Muslim woman praying outside the Friday
mosque, Isfahan. Islam became widespread after the Muslim
invasion and eventual defeat of Persia in the seventh century.
By the ninth century Islam was the majority religion.

at regular intervals five times a day. However stories remain of Zoroastrians being forced to convert at sword point. Until the ninth century, however, Zoroastrianism was still the majority religion. Scholarly Zoroastrian priests continued to write commentaries on the Avesta in Pahlavi (the Middle Persian language spoken by the Sassanians) adding to Zoroastrian knowledge. However Islam was firmly established. Ruling powers used a combination of persuasion, economic pressure, and force to convert everybody to Islam. By the late ninth century the Zoroastrian faithful were finding life increasingly hard.

In the 13th century Zoroastrians who remained faithful fled their homes to the cities of Yazd in central Iran and Kerman in southeast Iran, where they practiced their religion in secret. For a time the Muslims left them alone and they were able to live as craftspeople and farmers. However in the 16th century another wave of forced conversion took place. Zoroastrians moved to Isfahan, another city in central Iran, where they worked as laborers. In the early 17th century there was an Afghani invasion, followed not long after by an invasion when the Qajar dynasty seized power. In these two periods of warfare more than 100,000 Zoroastrians were killed.

ZOROASTRIAN FORTUNES IN THE NINETEENTH CENTURY

By the 19th century the plight of the Zoroastrians in Iran was dire indeed. Only about 12,000 were left. Although classi-

Islam Comes to Bukhara

After the Muslim invasion, the city of Bukhara remained steadfastly Zoroastrian, worshipping in their fire temples on their holy days. Three different times the Muslim ruler, Qutaybah ibn Muslim, made war on the city and converted the people, and all three times after he left they returned to Zoroastrianism. The fourth time Qutaybah made sure that there would be no backsliding. He made Zoroastrianism difficult for the people in every way possible. He ordered them to give half of their homes to Arabs who could watch and inform on them. He built mosques and destroyed fire temples. He severely punished people who broke Muslim religious laws and rewarded those who came to Friday prayer with gifts of money. Outside the city wealthy Zoroastrians in their villas still resisted. When soldiers called them to Friday prayer they threw stones at them from their rooftops. Finally they were overcome by military force . . .

(Adapted from Mary Boyce, *Textual Sources for the Study of Zoroastrianism*, 1984.)

fied as an official minority, they were persecuted. Muslim rulers levied a heavy tax called *jizya* on all non-Muslims. This tax effectively impoverished the Zoroastrian community. Iranian law heaped indignities on the vanishing population.

Zoroastrians were not allowed to travel and were forced to wear clothing made of undyed cloth. Laws banned them from touching food in the markets. They were forbidden to ride horses, and if they had the misfortune to be riding a donkey when a Muslim came by they had to get down and walk. Zoroastrian men were barred from wearing turbans, which made them instantly recognizable as *gabars* or "infidels"—nonbelievers—and subject to harassment and humiliation. Zoroastrians had no legal standing: A Muslim who killed a Zoroastrian faced no penalty. Yet in spite of overwhelming hardship Zoroastrians persisted in their religion. Despite Iranian society's efforts to wipe it out, Iranian Zoroastrianism continued.

Meanwhile in India the Parsi community of Zoroastrians who had relocated in India, was flourishing. In 1882 the Parsis sent an influential Parsi named Manekji Hataria to Iran to lobby the Qajar rulers on behalf of the Iranian Zoroastrians. Hataria's mission was at least partly successful. The repressive jizya was lifted and poverty eased. Soon after, education and better medical care became available. By the early 1900s Zoroastrians had begun to open businesses and improve their position in Iranian life. It took less than half a century for them to reverse hundreds of years of repression and become active in banking, education, engineering, and the professions.

The Parsis

Around the 10th century a group of devout Zoroastrians and their priests fled Persia to settle in India, where they became known as Parsis. Those who stayed behind all but disappeared as an influence on Iranian culture.

A 19th-century drawing of Zoroastrian priests and community members attending a Zoroastrian fire temple at Baku, Azerbaijan. Built around a fire caused by the escape of natural gas from the earth, this temple was rebuilt by Zoroastrians from India seeking to restore the ancient tradition of the religion in this area.

Meanwhile, in Iran at large corruption and weak government led to continual unrest. A series of uprisings caused the old Qajar dynasty to collapse in 1925. World War I (1914–18) only added to the confusion as power swung back and forth.

In 1925 a new dynasty headed by Reza Shah Pahlavi took control. Reza Shah was a strong leader who consolidated political power and brought about reforms. His policies were largely continued by his son, Mohammed Reza Pahlavi, who followed him on the Peacock Throne—the name of the Persian throne since the 18th century—in 1941.

Mohammed Reza Pahlavi, who ruled Iran from 1941 to 1979, and his wife Farah Dibah. Although Muslim, the shahs were sympathetic to the Zoroastrians, calling them "the true Persians" and using the example of Zoroastrian steadfastness to instill national pride.

Under the Pahlavi reign the fortunes of the Zoroastrians continued to improve. The shahs (rulers of Iran) moved to control Muslim religious influences and pointed to the small but durable band of Zoroastrians still surviving in Iran as the "true Persians." With the new pride in Zoroastrianism people whose families had been Muslim for centuries returned to the Zoroastrianism of their ancestors.

Pahlavi rule, however, had its own problems. As troubles multiplied, the shah's policies became harsher and the people more restless. In 1979 many opponents of the shah united under the Ayatollah Ruhollah Khomeini, a Muslim religious leader. He and his followers declared Iran to be an Islamic republic and established a new government based on the teachings of Islam.

With the return of a Muslim-ruled government many restrictions were placed on people's personal freedoms. This was especially the case for many Zoroastrians who had enjoyed improved status under the shah. The crackdown caused many of them to leave Iran. Citing the threat of religious persecution, they migrated to Britain, Australia, Canada, and the United States, among other countries. The Islamic Republic officially maintains Zoroastrianism as a "protected minority" in Iran and the persecution that the Zoroastrian community feared has not happened. Zoroastrians may not work for the government, for example, but they are respected in other areas of Iranian life. An unknown number of Iranian Muslims each year "revert" to Zoroastrianism. Although this is officially illegal there seem to have been no problems. Nevertheless, in a country overwhelmingly Muslim, educational and professional opportunities for Zoroastrians are somewhat limited and the threat of persecution remains.

CHAPTER 4

ZOROASTRIANISM IN INDIA: THE PARSIS

After the Arab invasion in 642 C.E. life was increasingly harsh for Zoroastrians. In 651 the Arabs overthrew the last Persian emperor, Yazdegard III, and took over the Persian throne. Over the next 200 years the Muslim rulers made conversion to Islam a priority. For those who would not give up their Zoroastrian religion the penalties multiplied.

A group of Zoroastrian priests and believers abandoned their homes and their temple. Carrying the consecrated fire with them they withdrew to the Khorasan Mountains in northeast Iran, where they formed a community. For a time they lived peacefully but eventually they were discovered and persecuted there as well. They left the mountains and settled in the town of Hormuz, near the Persian Gulf. However once again they were harassed. Finally one of their priests advised them that if they were to survive as a Zoroastrian community they would have to leave Persia.

The Zoroastrians sailed from Hormuz to Diu, an island off the coast of western India. They stayed in Diu for a time usually given as 19 years. Then, following the advice of one of their priests they set sail again, this time for the Indian state of Gujarat.

Looking across the Indian city of Mumbai, a city that has historically had a strong Zoroastrian presence and influence.

Far out in the Gulf the Zoroastrians met a terrible storm that threatened to swamp the boats and take them all to the bottom. Battered by winds and waves and in desperate fear for their lives, the travelers prayed to Ahura Mazda for a safe harbor and promised to build a holy fire temple if they reached land alive.

The winds subsided and they landed in Sanjan, a port north of what is now the city of Mumbai (formerly called Bombay). The actual date of their migration is uncertain. It is usually given as 936 but sometimes earlier. Probably there were a number of migrations through the ninth and 10th centuries.

PARSI MIGRATION

After the Muslim invasion, devout Zoroastrians first fled to the Khorasan Mountains. Persecuted there, they settled in Hormuz, but the persecution continued. Finally they set sail for India via the Persian Gulf. They first landed in Diu, where they lived for 19 years. Then they moved again, landing in Sanjan in the state of Gujarat. Gradually they spread to Surat and Navsari, where they established Zoroastrian communities.

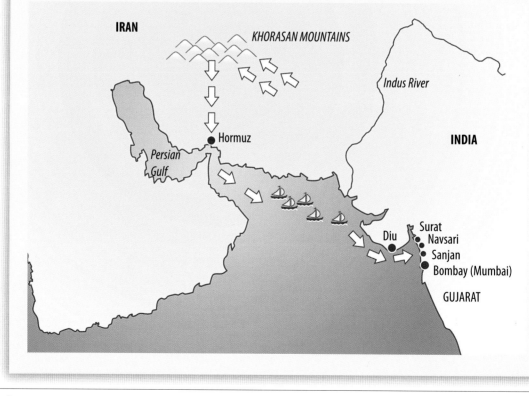

SEEKING ASYLUM

According to tradition the chief priest, or *dastur,* approached the local Hindu ruler, Jadi Rana, for asylum. He asked for only three things: the freedom to practice their religion, the freedom to bring up their children according to their own custom, and a small piece of land.

The Parsis, the Zoroastrians of India, tell that Jadi Rana offered the Zoroastrians a pitcher of milk that was full to the brim by way of explaining that his realm was already crowded. The Zoroastrian leader added a pinch of sugar to the milk to suggest that the Zoroastrians would fit in and enrich the country. Jadi Rana permitted the Zoroastrians to stay on the condition that they agreed to five conditions. The Datsur agreed to these terms and the new arrivals were granted the land they had requested. They immediately set about building a consecrated fire temple of the highest grade, an *atash behram* in which to place their sacred fire. The ritual implements required to consecrate the fire were brought from Persia and only then was it possible to create the sacred fire for the first time in India.

JADI RANA'S CONDITIONS

When the first Zoroastrians left Persia they sailed down the Persian Gulf from Hormuz. They first landed in Diu on the northwest coast of India. When the Zoroastrians moved down the coast to Sanjan, the local Hindu ruler, Jadi Rana, granted the Zoroastrians' requests for asylum on five conditions:

They must educate the ruler about the Zoroastrian religion.

They must give up their Persian language and speak only Gujarati, the local language.

The women must adopt Indian dress and wear the sari.

The men must give up their weapons.

They must agree to hold their weddings only in the evening so as not to conflict with Hindu ceremonies.

LIFE IN INDIA

Over the next centuries the Zoroastrian community flourished. They kept to themselves and did not seek converts, but the community grew steadily. One reason was that they had very large families. They made their living as farmers and merchants. Gradually they spread out from Sanjan into the surrounding areas. Wherever they went they built fire temples and worshipped Ahura Mazda. In towns along the coast Parsis took up shipbuilding and other trades. Hardworking and scrupulously honest, they won the respect of the people with whom they worked.

Around 1297 Muslim invaders advanced on the Sanjan area. A group of 1,400 Zoroastrian men joined the Hindu army to fight off the attack. After days of bloody fighting in which the battle seesawed back and forth, Sanjan fell to the Muslims. The Zoroastrians fled to the nearby mountain of Bahrot. For the next 12 years they preserved their sacred fire in the caves of Bahrot and then moved it to a village called Bansda, where it stayed for 14 years. In 1419 priests moved the holy fire to the town of Navsari. It remained there for 300 years.

A Parsi woman kisses her daughter at a fire temple in Ahmadabad, India, on the occasion of the Parsi new year in 2007.

From 1737 to 1742 the sacred fire was taken to the seaport cities of Bulsar (known today as Valsad) and Surat. In 1742 the Zoroastrians of the town Udvada built an atash behram there and moved the sacred fire to a permanent home. By this time the Zoroastrians had been in India for more than 700 years.

Meanwhile Parsis established themselves in business and trade. They were trading with the Portuguese in the 16th century and by the mid-1700s Parsi merchants had traveled to China to establish trade links there. In spite of their cosmopolitan contacts, however, they held to their Zoroastrian religious tradition.

KEEPING THE FAITH: THE RIVAYATS

The Parsi community spoke Gujarati, the language of the part of India in which they lived, but they still used the language of the Avestan communitiy, Pahlavi as a ritual language. Priests learned the ancient texts by heart, although by now few people fully understood their meaning. Even though they had given up their language and many of their Persian customs for Indian ones, the Parsis still looked to the Zoroastrian priests as the authorities on their religion. Through the 16th century they corresponded with the priests of Kirman and Yazd, the last centers of Zoroastrianism left in Iran. The high priest, or *dastur-an dastur,* of Yazd, in particular, who had gathered a religious community of priests around him, was considered to be the best source of religious knowledge. The Parsis wrote to the *dastur* with their questions on matters of orthodox belief and ritual and received answers. The *Parsi Rivayats,* or "letters," span nearly a century and became part of Zoroastrian literature.

THE PANCHAYAT

Although Parsi religious tradition was strong they did adopt certain Hindu social customs. By the late 17th century Parsi society was organized along the lines of a Hindu caste, led by a *panchayat,* a group of community leaders. The panchayat settled disputes and made rulings about social issues such as family quarrels, property arguments, and divorce settlements. They also managed community property and trusts. Priests handled religious matters, however.

Since the early 1700s, the British had been exercising commercial and political power in India and by the early 19th century unofficially ruled much of the country. By 1858 India had become officially part of the vast British Empire. The British Raj—a Hindu word meaning "reign"—controlled India for the next 90 years.

When the British took control of India Parsis were already well established in the city of Mumbai. They had begun moving to the city to trade with the Portuguese in the 15th century. By 1672

An early-20th-century portrait of a Parsi family in Mumbai. The city became the main center of Zoroastrian religion in India.

they had a temple and a *dakhma,* a structure for disposing of their dead, there. In the late 1700s drought in Gujarat made farming unprofitable and many more Parsis migrated to Mumbai. Always industrious, they found jobs in business and banking. The Parsis were not bound by the Hindu caste system, which made upward mobility difficult for Hindus. They established themselves quickly and rose in importance in Indian cultural and economic life.

PARSIS UNDER BRITISH RULE

Parsis were popular with British employers because of their truthfulness and reliability. Their religion taught them to live fully in society and to fight worldly evils such as illness and poverty. What better way than to succeed economically, to have the money and power to do good in the world?

Besides, Parsis had always kept to themselves. They had maintained their Persian identity and never felt strongly Indian. Strangers in India themselves, even after hundreds of years, they had no reason to resent British rule. On the contrary they welcomed the opportunities the British offered in education and business. They were quick to study and learn English, which made them even more desirable to the British. From the British standpoint the Parsis were welcome as both workers and friends. The Hindus, who neither drank wine nor ate meat, refused British hospitality. The Parsis were pleasant and sociable. Parsis soon gained economic strength that was considerably greater than their numbers in the Indian population would suggest was possible. Many owned their own prosperous businesses. Some credit the Parsis with having a special genius for business, but more likely their success was driven by the strong work ethic of Zoroastrianism and their respect for learning.

In general the Parsis thrived, but they did encounter difficulties. In 1851 Indian

WOMEN IN PARSI SOCIETY

Parsi women also benefited from British rule. The British offered educational opportunities for women that had not been widely available before, and Parsis enrolled their daughters in record numbers. Although Iranian and later Indian society had placed restrictions on women, Zoroastrianism placed women on a par with men in matters of religion and education. Parsi families welcomed the chance to educate their daughters.

Muslims objected to something in a Parsi publication, and riots broke out. Parsi homes and businesses were damaged and looted. A similar event occurred in 1874 when Muslims attacked Parsi fire temples.

BUSINESS, SCIENCE, AND ARTS

On the whole, however, the Parsis prospered. They were hard-working and quick to adopt new ideas. A number of Parsis amassed fortunes in such areas as shipbuilding, international trading, textiles, iron and steel, and engineering. It was a Parsi, Jehangir Ratan D. Tata, who won the first pilot's license ever issued in India and founded India's first air service, Tata Aviation, which later became Air India. Parsis established the first wireless service, which linked India to Britain by radio for the first time.

Parsi friends and family gathered for a meal. The Parsi community supports religious and educational equality for women.

A Parsi scientist was responsible for India's atomic energy program. Parsis founded the Bombay (Mumbai) Symphony. Parsis also excelled in areas such as law and education.

PARSI PHILANTHROPY

At the same time Parsis were quick to reach out to those less fortunate than themselves. Along with their reputation as shrewd but honest businesspeople, they became known for their generous giving to charitable causes. Zoroastrianism teaches that anyone who fights the evils of society such as illness, poverty, and ignorance is working with Ahura Mazda toward perfecting the world. Parsis became known for philanthropy. The most successful Parsi businesspeople were also the most generous. Parsi money built much of modern Mumbai. Besides erecting more than 160 fire temples they donated primary funding to house the poor and to build many hospitals, schools, libraries, and institutes of science and art. When disaster struck anywhere in the country Parsis were among the first to send aid. They provided scholarships and built cultural halls and museums, not just for Parsis, but open to all.

PARSIS IN MODERN TIMES

For more than 50 years before India gained independence, the Indian National Movement had been trying to win freedom from British rule. A number of Parsis were active in the movement, both as elected officials who spoke for Indian nationalism and as spokespeople for Indian freedom. Perhaps even more important than political efforts, Parsi business and industry served to help India become economically strong, making independence possible. India won its independence at the close of World War II (1939–45). At that time the country was partitioned into India, which today is strongly Hindu, and Pakistan, which is mainly Muslim.

With the withdrawal of the British from India, the Parsis lost some of their favored status. The Hindu National Party became the ruling political power. Parsis were once again only a small minority in a huge country. Moreover the partition of India, which took place between 1947 and 1949, divided the already small Parsi population in India by making the Parsis in the north Pakistani citizens. However Parsis still had considerable economic strength and energy. Today they participate in every aspect of Indian business and culture. Parsis have immigrated to North America, Europe, and Australia in search of educational opportunities and jobs in technical fields. Wherever they go they work to maintain their commitment to their religion.

IDENTITY AND INTERMARRIAGE

Parsis are and have always been exclusive. To conservative Parsis their faith is a God-given birthright that cannot be acquired from the outside. Parsis consider themselves a distinct ethnic group. According to a 1906 ruling by the Bombay High Court, people who are not born of two Parsi parents or who come to Zoroastrianism from outside the religion may become Zoroastrians, but they can never consider themselves Parsis. Parsis are only those people who are descended from the original Persian immigrants. The only exception is that the children of Parsi fathers by non-Parsi mothers may be accepted into the faith. The children of Parsi mothers by non-Parsi fathers may not. Only "true" Parsis—that is, active believers who were born of two Parsi parents—may enter the presence of a consecrated fire or observe the highest Zoroastrian rites. Many Parsis feel deeply that marrying only within the faith is one of the main things that has kept their religion alive for more than 3,000 years, and permitting intermarriage weakens the religion.

ZUBIN MEHTA

The conductor Zubin Mehta is a Parsi, born in Mumbai, India. Mehta grew up in a musical home; his father was one of the founders of the Bombay Symphony. He first intended to be a doctor and began a premed course, but soon switched to music. After studying in Mumbai and Vienna, Mehta went on to win first prize in an international competition in Liverpool, England, when he was 22. Mehta has conducted orchestras around the world, including the Philadelphia Orchestra, the Montreal Symphony, the Vienna Philharmonic Orchestra, and the Metropolitan Opera Orchestra in New York. He performs regularly as guest conductor with the Vienna Philharmonic, the Berlin Philharmonic, and the Orchestre de Paris. He is the Director for Life of the Israel Philharmonic Orchestra and the Artistic Director of Maggio Musicale Fiorentino in Florence, Italy.

Zubin Mehta conducting an orchestra.

India's prime minister at the time, Indira Gandhi, far right, stands with her family in New Delhi, September 17, 1973. From left, Mrs. Gandhi's daughter-in-law Sonia carrying grandaughter Priyanki; sons Sanjay and Rajiv; and grandson Rahul. Indira Gandhi's husband, Feroze Gandhi, belonged to a Parsi family. Parsis still participate in Indian politics and many hold high government positions in spite of their small numbers in Indian society.

MAINTAINING TRADITIONAL FAITH

The basic debate is one that asks: "Who is a Parsi?" For some a Parsi is one who belongs primarily to an ethnic group—that is, Zoroastrians of the Iranian diaspora. For others a Parsi is anyone who follows a way of life dedicated to good thoughts, words, and deeds in accord with the spirit of the Master.

In today's world modern demands have challenged traditional ways of defining people and their ethnic and religious identities. The Parsis of India have experienced this challenge even more than many other religious communities. They have the largest concentration of Zoroastrian believers in one place. Yet in today's world, they are still only .01 percent of the Indian population and need to find new means of preservation. They must work to maintain a traditional faith and to preserve the number of dedicated faithful followers. In a greatly changing world they must also ask themselves what measures must they take to guarantee their survival and growth in such new and demanding circumstances.

CHAPTER 5

THE AVESTA: THE ZOROASTRIAN SCRIPTURE

The Zoroastrian scripture is the Avesta. Its contents were created over many centuries reaching back into prehistory. The oldest part of the Avesta was composed in Gathic Avestan, the language of the prophet Zarathustra. The part of the Avesta in Gathic includes the 17 hymns or psalms composed by Zarathustra himself. Other sections of the Avesta are written in a slightly later but still very ancient form of Avestan that scholars call "Young Avestan" to distinguish it from Gathic Avestan.

Traditional Zoroastrians consider their sacred scriptures to have immense spiritual power. Not only do they teach truth, but merely to speak the Avestan words aloud or to hear them spoken by a priest is a special blessing that helps to fight evil and furthers the cause of Truth in the world. From the scriptures come the liturgy and daily prayers of Zoroastrians.

HISTORY OF THE AVESTA

The Avesta began as an oral document memorized and recited by priests. In Zarathustra's place and time writing was unknown, and priestly training generally required such feats of memory.

Zoroastrian priests during a prayer ritual at the Zoroastrian temple in London, England. Zoroastrian associations throughout the United Kingdom maintain contact with each other and with the international community.

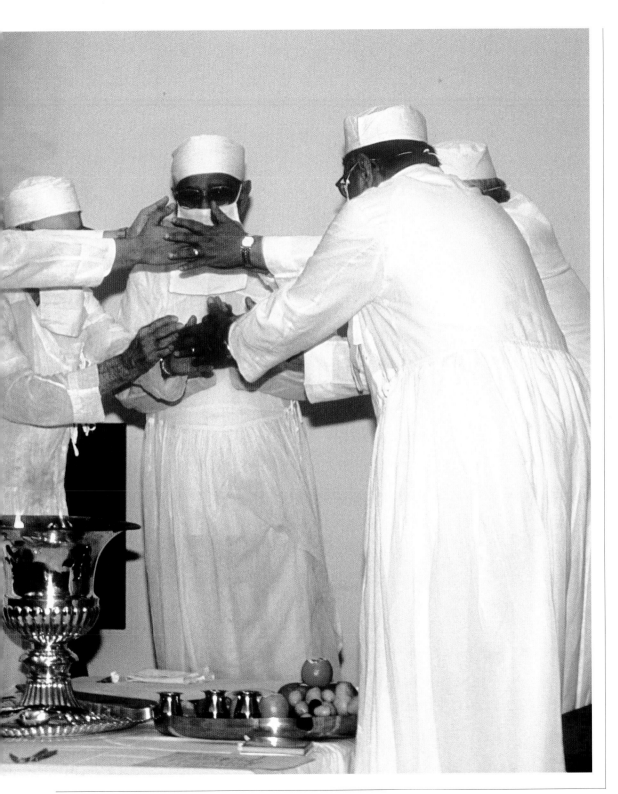

Avestan	Pahlavi
Ahura Mazda	Ohrmazd, Hormazd
Spenta Mainyu	Spenag Menog
Angra Mainyu	Ahriman
Asha	Ardvahist
Vohu Mana	Vahman
Spenta Armaity	Aspandarmad
Khshathra Vairya	Shehrevar
Haurvatat	Khordad
Ameratat	Amardad
Mithra	Meher, Mehr

Religious belief and ritual were never written down. Even when writing first appeared, it was used for record keeping and trade, not for composing literature, which was an oral art.

No one knows when scribes began to collect Zarathustra's songs and commit them to writing. Tradition holds that in 330 B.C.E., when the Greek general Alexander burned the palace at Persepolis and its library, one of the treasures he destroyed was a complete copy of the Avesta, written in gold on 12,000 goatskins. So total was the destruction that it will never be known whether such a document actually existed. In any event the effect of the Greek army's devastation on Zoroastrian learning was the same. Whatever Avestan writings were there were scattered and burned. In addition a great many Zoroastrian priests were slaughtered by Alexander's army. The Avestan passages the priests had committed to memory died with them, never to be completely recalled.

THE GREAT AVESTA

Almost 400 years later, in the first century C.E. when the Parthians were in power, a ruler set his scribes to collecting the scattered pieces of the Avesta. The work continued under the Sassanians. Through the fourth and fifth centuries C.E. they collected volumes of material that they assembled in a "Great Avesta." The work they produced included not only all the Avestan texts, but translations and explanations of them in Pahlavi, their language. Copies were placed in the libraries of the leading fire temples.

In the seventh century an invasion by the Arabs swept Persia, dethroning the Sassanians. Zoroastrianism suffered great losses. Scholar-priests continued the work of creating the Zand, commentary and translations of the Avesta, written in Pahlavi, for at least two more centuries. In the end, though, invasions by the Turks and the Mongols completed the destruction begun by the Arabs. Zoroastrian temples were burned and their libraries with them. Not a single complete copy of the Great Avesta survived. However, enough of the ancient Avestan writings remained that they could once again be collected into the Avesta known today. It is probably about one-fourth of the original.

FIRST EUROPEAN TRANSLATION

Following the Arab conquest the language, script, and religion of Persia changed completely. Zoroastrianism all but disappeared from the world's consciousness for the next thousand years. In 1755 a French scholar named Abraham Anquetil-Duperon came across Zoroastrianism in India. He published a translation of the Avesta in France in 1771. His efforts brought a knowledge of the Avesta to the modern world.

The Zand

The Sassanians (226–641) were responsible for collecting as much as they could of the "Lost Avesta." These were the parts of the Avesta that had presumably been destroyed by the Greeks but that had survived in the oral tradition. The Lost Avesta passages provide important clues to the contents of the original Avesta. These, along with other Zoroastrian writings, they assembled in what is called the Zand.

THE YASNA

The Avesta opens with the Yasna or "sacrifice." It contains the Zoroastrian liturgy, the formal words spoken by priests during worship, including the creed of belief of all Zoroastrians and formal invocations for priests to speak as they perform various rituals. Parts of the Yasna form the daily prayers of all Zoroastrians. Some of the Yasna liturgy, such as the Yasna Haptanhaiti, is composed in Gathic Avestan dating to Zarathustra's time. Much however is in Young Avestan, as Zoroastrian liturgy probably developed over the centuries following Zarathustra's lifetime, when Gathic was no longer spoken.

For Zoroastrians a central part of the Yasna is the 17 Gathic hymns that are the actual words of Zarathustra. These 17 Gathas or psalms occupy a very special place in Zoroastrianism. All Zoroastrian doctrine and belief are based on them.

CONTENTS OF THE AVESTA

The sacred scripture of the Avesta is in six parts:

Yasna, "sacrifice, worship." The main liturgical text. It includes the Gathas, the fundamental teachings of Zarathustra.

Visperad, "All the Lords." A liturgical text invoking Zoroastrian heavenly beings, used on Zoroastrian holy days.

Yashts, hymns of praise to Zoroastrian angels, or *yazatas*. The Yashts praise many of the deities from Iranian religion before Zarathustra's reforms.

Vendidad, a priestly code dealing mainly with rituals, regulations, and purification.

Khorda Avesta, containing minor texts like Nyayesh, Gah, and other short prayers, sometimes from other parts of the Avesta, used as prayers and invocations by both priests and laypeople.

Fragments of the Lost Avesta, prayers, invocations, and blessings.

THE GATHAS

Zarathustra composed the Gathas at various times throughout his life, and he probably composed many more than the 17 in the Yasna. The Gathas that have come down to us are probably only fragments of Zarathustra's message. However they are enough to glimpse the power of his preaching and his poetic style, and to understand the vision he had of Ahura Mazda and the Good Religion.

The Gathas probably survived in their original form because they were poems. Their rhythm and meter made them easier to memorize than prose, and also harder to change. Zarathustra's own words provide one of the best ways to understand the fundamental beliefs of Zoroastrianism.

No one knows exactly in what order these hymns were composed, although there are some clues within them. Later scholars organized the 17 Gathas believed to be by Zarathustra into five groups within the Yasna, according to their meter:

Ahunavaiti Gatha—Ys. 28–34
Ushtavaiti Gatha—Ys. 43–46
Spenta Mainyu Gatha—Ys. 47–50
Vohu Khshathra Gatha—Ys. 51
Vahishto Ishti Gatha—Ys. 53

In these passages Zarathustra lays down the basic principles of Zoroastrian faith, although not in a systematic or doctrinaire way. The Gathas are expressions of Zarathustra's belief in and personal experience with God. Some are songs of praise to Ahura Mazda; others are prayers and thanksgiving; and some are dialogues with Ahura Mazda concerning universal questions of the meaning of life and how it is to be lived.

AHUNAVAITI: YS. 28–34

The Ahunavaiti Gathas open with a hymn to Ahura Mazda in which Zarathustra prays for the gifts of righteousness and wisdom, that he may spread joy in the world.

The next hymn, Ys. 29, is known as "The Lament of the Cow." Zarathustra composes his hymn in the sorrowful voice of the cow, which is laboring under warfare and unrest. For Zarathustra and his listeners the Cow represents the pastoral life being destroyed by warfare and violence. Its voice is the soul of creation. The lament is more touching coming from this poor voiceless creature that must suffer because of human greed and cruelty. The soul of the cow cries to Ahura Mazda

Hymn to Ahura Mazda found in the Ahunavaiti Gatha of the Yasna:

In humble adoration, with hands outstretched.
I pray to thee, O Mazda
Through Thy benevolent Spirit,
Vouchsafe to me in this hour of joy
All righteousness of action,
all wisdom of the Good Mind,
That I may thereby bring joy to the Soul of Creation

—Ys. 28.1

Primal Spirits

*In the beginning there were
two Primal Spirits,
Twins simultaneously active,
These are the Good and the Evil,
in thought, and in word, and in deed.
Between these two, let the wise
one choose aright,
Be good, not base.*

Evil destroys and it brings those who choose it nothing but misery. Those who choose good, however, are helping to move the world toward perfection and themselves toward eternal joy.

for a protector. Ahura Mazda then turns to Zarathustra, "The one who alone has hearkened to my command." The soul has doubts. It asked for someone powerful, and Zarathustra is neither a great king nor a great warrior, but a humble man. Even Zarathustra is uncertain. Ahura Mazda prevails, however, and Zarathustra sets out on his mission.

In Ys. 30.3 Zarathustra begins to lay out his message to followers. He offers them the hope of heaven through following the path of Truth (Asha). He tells his listeners that there has always been evil in the world but that people have within them the wisdom to choose good over evil.

Cattle were supremely important in Zarathustra's culture. There was no part of them that could not be used—milk, meat, hide, bones, manure. People were enormously dependent on their cattle and felt a great kinship with them.

In Ys. 34 Zarathustra addresses Ahura Mazda, asking the Lord to confirm his mission. This Gatha was probably written when Zarathustra was in middle age, after the religion had been adopted by Kai Vishtaspa and his court. The new faith was slow in catching on. Zarathustra tells Ahura Mazda that his followers are following Asha, the path of Truth. Yet people still practice the old religion and Zarathustra asks Ahura Mazda for reassurance.

USHTAVAITI: YS. 43–46

In the Ushtavaiti Gathas Zarathustra asks Ahura Mazda questions having to do with the meaning of existence—questions that are central to all religious thought. In the version of the Avesta that exists today Zarathustra answers some questions, but many are left open for followers to ponder.

Zarathustra goes on to ask many other questions of the human heart such as how best to make the soul take the Good to itself, how best to praise Ahura Mazda, how the religion can be made to prosper, and how a righteous person can be told from an unrighteous one. In questions such as these he deals with the thorny issues that have plagued humankind through all religious history. Finally he asks how he may achieve the perfection of the Good Mind that he so earnestly seeks.

In Ys. 45 Zarathustra delivers a sermon to his followers. He reminds them of the conflict between good and evil, which can "never agree." He has come to bring the message of Ahura Mazda, with the warning that for those who do not follow it there will be eternal misery. What is best in life is to follow the spirit of Truth, Asha, and to live according to the Good Mind and good actions.

Seeking Reassurance

Zarathustra, concerned that people still practice the old religion, turns to Ahura Mazda for help:

What are thy commandments, and what dost thou desire, O Mazda?
What of invocation, what of worship?
Speak forth, my Lord, that I may hear thee!
That I may know what will bestow on us Thy Blessed rewards. Teach me through the Good-Mind and the noble Path of Truth and Right.

—Ys. 34.12

Even in his questioning Zarathustra is certain that all will be revealed through the Good Mind, so that humankind and Ahura Mazda can work together to further Ahura Mazda's plan.

The Creator of Truth

This I ask Thee, tell me truly, O Ahura;
In the beginning, who was the father and
creator of Asha, the Truth?
Who determined the paths of the
sun and stars?
Who, but Thee, so arranged the moon to
wax and wane?
This, O Mazda, and much more, I fain
would know.

—Ys. 44.3

The answer to the question seems obvious: Ahura Mazda. However by posing the thought as a question Zarathustra invites his listeners to answer for themselves. He also links Truth with such natural phenomena as the sun, moon, and stars, implying that it is a fundamental principle of all existence.

Making a Bond

In the final verse of Yasna 45 Zarathustra promises a personal relationship with Ahura Mazda:

Whoso shuns the evil-liars and those
who shun the Lord
Whoso reveres Him, the most High,
through the holy faith of his
appointed Savior,
To him, O Mazda, Thou shalt be a
friend, even brother and father!

—Ys. 45.11

Those who do this shall be blessed with perfection and immortality.

In the next Gatha of this group (Ys. 46) Zarathustra reflects on his earlier life and difficulties. He recalls being deserted and rejected. At the time he wondered aloud why his followers were so few and his message so little heard. Yet as the Gatha continues it is clear that Zarathustra was never close to giving up. He knows that the way of Asha is the Good Life and that those who refuse to follow it will come to grief in the end. He calls upon the people who rejected him to come to the Right.

SPENTA MAINYU: YS. 47–50

The next group of psalms is short. It takes its name from the spirit of Truth. Zarathustra speaks to Ahura Mazda and to his followers. The tone of the poem suggests that these were not easy times. There are hints of political unrest. Zarathustra expresses the hope that the righteous may win out over the unrighteous, and that the people be ruled by those who know how to rule well, not evil rulers. "When shall happy life in peaceful pastures come to us through good rule?" he asks (Ys. 48.11). Yet at the end he foresees a time when leaders appointed by Ahura Mazda will come to take away violence and bring Truth and Justice.

VOHU KHSHATHRA: YS. 51

In this Gatha, which relates to Ahura Mazda's power and might, Zarathustra returns

A Zoroastrian priest reading hymns from the Gathas. The 17 hymns of the Gathas were composed by Zarathustra.

to the theme of what awaits the wicked, a trial by fire and molten metal that will destroy them. The souls of the wicked will be turned back at the Chinvat Bridge, the Bridge of the Separator where souls of the dead meet judgement, because they have wandered from the path of Truth. He mentions those who have become enlightened—his cousin Maidhyoimaongha, the king Vishtaspa, and the members of the king's court, Frashaoshtra and Jamaspa—and asks that Ahura Mazda give them, and him, salvation.

VAHISHTO ISHTI: YS. 53

This Gatha tells of the wedding of Pouruchista, Zarathustra's youngest daughter, to Jamaspa, an official in the court of Vishtaspa. Some scholars believe that this Gatha was composed by a follower of Zarathustra rather than by Zarathustra himself. However it does provide a glimpse into everyday life in Zarathustra's time.

Although they are only a part of the body of psalms composed by Zarathustra, the Gathas form a unified picture of his message. People can find salvation by serving Ahura Mazda through the goodness of their lives and hearts. Those who follow the path of righteousness will find joy and contentment in this world and after death, but those who are evil will perish.

INTERPRETING THE TEXTS

Zoroastrian scholars continually debate the exact meanings of different passages in the Gathas. Zarathustra was preaching to people who understood not only his language but references to the Iranian gods and religious practices. As in all poetry the language may be compressed and the meaning difficult to interpret. Zoroastrians may spend their whole lives trying to understand

UNDERSTANDING THE GATHAS

The language in which the older portions of the Avesta is written, Gathic Avestan, is the only known example of this particular dialect. It survived in the oral tradition through centuries because people believed that the sounds of the Gathic words were especially pleasing to Ahura Mazda. Because of its great age and obscure dialect, the Avesta is notoriously difficult to translate and to understand. Gathic words often had a number of meanings. Many different interpretations are possible, even likely. For example, *Sraosha* is the name of an angel or a characteristic of Ahura Mazda, but may also mean "conscience" or "obedience." Much depends on context and the skill of the translator.

Zoroastrian priests reading prayers from the Avesta, sacred scripture, during an inter-faith gathering in Nepal to highlight practical and educational environmental work being carried out in religious traditions including the Zoroastrian community.

what Zarathustra meant. However for them the challenge of understanding is one of the things that keeps their religion fresh and alive.

THE VISPERAD

This part of the Avesta is a long liturgical text that is based on the Yasna and Vendidad, a priestly code, with additional prayers. It is used to celebrate the great holy days, or *gahambars,* of Zoroastrianism.

THE YASHTS

The Yashts are 21 hymns of praise to *yazatas*—angels and other divine beings. They are composed in Young Avestan, indicating that they came into the literature after the Yasna, but their content goes back to a much earlier time. Many Yashts praise earlier gods and goddesses of nature such as Mithra, a deity of ancient Iran who reappears in Zoroastrianism as the deity of Heavenly Light. Another being praised in the Yashts is Sraosha, the first of the heavenly beings to worship Ahura Mazda and later one of the deities to help the faithful across the Chinvat Bridge, along with Mithra and Rashnu, the spirit of Justice.

Other Yashts praise such spirits as Conscience, Victory, the Wind, Sun, and Rain, Righteousness, the *haoma* plant, and the geographical features of the Iranian world. There are also hymns to the fravashis, the guardian spirits of all living beings. The Hormazd Yasht lists the 72 names of Ahura Mazda, "the sustainer, maintainer, creator and nourisher," which may be recited to guard against evil.

The Yashts

These hymns of praise suggest a time when Zoroastrianism was incorporating elements of the old Iranian religion. In praising such deities as the Wind, Victory, and the Rain Star they connect Zoroastrianism to the ancient Iranian religion before Zarathustra.

THE VENDIDAD

The Vendidad contains the priestly code of Zoroastrianism. It is mainly concerned with ritual and physical purity. It is not certain whether Zarathustra himself laid down rules for purity, but spiritual purity

THE NAMES OF AHURA MAZDA

From a litany from the Hormazad Yasht of the Avesta

I am the sustainer, maintainer, and the reformer of my creations.
I am both the creator and nourisher [thereof],
    and I am possessed of the faculty of premonition.
I am the most bountiful spirit,
I am the giver of the greatest blessings of good health,
    through my name,
I am the most perfect giver of the greatest good health,
    through my name,
I am by name Athravan (the keeper of the sacred flame),
I am by name the most perfect Athravan,
I am by name Ahura, the creator of life,
I am by name Mazda, the omniscient,
I am by name holy righteousness,
I am by name the possessor of the highest degree of
    divine righteousness,
I am by name, glory,
By name I am the holder of the greatest glory,
I am by name, a complete seer,
I am by name the most complete seer,
By (my) name, "I Exist,". . .
I am by name the provider of bounties,
I am by name the master-thought, that provides bounties,
I am by name the wielder of divine power, glory and will,
I am by name the glorious wielder of divine authority . . .
I am by name the one opposed to destructiveness
    and wickedness,
I am by name the one who overcomes opposition of evil,
I am by name the one who overcomes all manner
    of obstacles,
I am by name the fashioner of all creations,
I am by name illimitable radiance,
I am by name the complete distributor of my universal radiance.
I am by name the unextinguishable light of the universe.

was important in his teaching. In order to be spiritually pure one had to be physically pure. This meant respecting the elements of fire, water, air, and earth; maintaining personal cleanliness; and avoiding pollution. The most serious form of pollution was that of coming in contact with death, and the Vendidad presents rules for purifying those who handle the dead. Purification rites help to keep away the forces of evil. There are also remedies for offenses such as causing physical harm to another person or a good animal.

The early chapters of the Vendidad do not deal with ritual purity. The first tells how Ahura Mazda creates 16 happy lands only to have them attacked by Angra Mainyu. The second tells how the Aryan (Iranian) people traveled south into Iran, in search of grazing land for their animals. Chapter 3 describes the joy of the earth when righteous people settle and plant crops upon it, and its sorrow when evil attacks. People are urged to undo evil to please the earth.

MINOR TEXTS OF THE AVESTA

The minor texts of the Avesta is a section of the Avesta that contains the Nyayesh and the Gah. These are prayers recited during the regular prayer cycle by both priests and laypeople. The five Nyayesh are addressed to the Sun and Moon as symbols of Ahura Mazda; to Mithra, the spirit of Light; and to Water and Fire. The five Gah are similar. Each day is divided into five gah, or periods, for prayer. The Gah are prayers Zoroastrians recite five times each day. Both the Nyayesh and the Gah contain invocations and passages from the Gathas and the Yashts.

Another collection of prayers in this section is referred to as the Khorda Avesta or "Little Avesta." It combines sections from the other texts in the Avesta, both in Avestan and the later Middle Persian, or Pahlavi, languages. This combined text is a prayer book for everyday use by Zoroastrians. All copies of the Khorda Avesta contain the same basic materials, but sometimes in different order. Some also include prayers in a more modern language such as Persian or Gujarati, the language spoken by the Parsis.

The Khorda Avesta first came into popular use in the 19th century when the holy texts became widely available.

FRAGMENTS OF THE AVESTA

The Great Avesta of the Sassanian era (226–641) contained not only the sacred Avestan scriptures, but also many other texts. It included stories and legends of the Prophet's life from oral sources, books of Zoroastrian law, tales of creation and the end of the world, and all that was known of science, astronomy, and the universe at the time. All copies of this huge work were lost in the Arab invasion and later invasions by the Turks and the Mongols. Fragments of the Great Avesta that did survive have been collected into a small section of today's Avesta.

THE PAHLAVI ZAND

The Avesta of today is sometimes called the Zand (or Zend) Avesta or the Avesta-Zand. The word *zand* refers to explanations, commentaries, and translations. Commentary was probably always a part of the Avesta but the earliest notes have been lost. The Zand known today, written in Pahlavi, is from Sassanian times. The Sassanians produced a great body of Zand. Scholar-priests continued to research and write for a long time after the Arab invasion, well into the ninth century. One of the later texts is the *Denkard,* which summarizes the contents of the Avesta from beginning to end.

The Zand is often the only clue to what the Avesta included before wars and invasions destroyed it. It is immensely helpful in reconstructing Avestan history and in showing how the Avesta has been interpreted and explained over many centuries.

THE BUNDAHISHN

One part of the Lost Avesta that appears in the Zand is the *Bundahishn,* or "Creation." The Bundahishn tells the story of the creation of the world. Ahura Mazda created the first man, Gayomart. From him came the first couple, from whom came the races of humankind. When they assumed human form Ahura Mazda

Stone reliefs of courtly officials from the ancient palace of
Darius at Persepolis in Iran. Evidence from the site shows that
Darius followed the Zoroastrian religion.

taught them the principles of the Mazday-azni religion, the forerunner of Zoroastrianism: Think good thoughts, speak good words, do good deeds, and do not worship the demons. (G.Bd. 14.11) The story of creation, like the other myths and legends of prehistory that appear in the Zand with ritual and historical fact, is an important link in a continuous chain of truth in the consciousness of Zoroastrian people.

The book also tells the nature of the divine beings, the Amesha Spentas, and details the end of the world. According to the Bundahishn, at the end of time the earth will be covered with molten metal. The wise and just, led by their savior, will walk through the metal as if it were warm milk, while the evil will be consumed in it. When the earth has been purified by fire all the dead will rise and live in peace and harmony in Ahura Mazda's perfected world.

Historical Inscriptions

In addition to the Avesta and Gathas, there are also some non-Zoroastrian writings that could serve as sources for the study of its teachings. These are the inscriptions dating from the time of the Persian kings Cyrus (559–529 B.C.E.) and Darius (522–486 B.C.E.) that speak of a god Ahuramazda. However the Zoroastrian orthodoxy of these inscriptions has been challenged. The reason it has been challenged is because Cyrus's mausoleum indicates entombment, which was not in keeping with the Zoroastrian customs. These other writings, then, seem more appropriate for studying the history and development of Zoroastrianism rather than helping people to understand the message of its religious founder.

THE IMPORTANCE OF THE AVESTA

The Avesta is one of the world's oldest scriptures. Its blend of ritual and inspiration contains all that Zoroastrians have needed to follow their faith and live according to its precepts for more than 3,000 years. Although it is known today only in part, it speaks to people in modern times much as it did in Zarathustra's day. It remains the essential guide to the "Good Religion" that Zoroastrians rely on in their devotions and in their daily lives.

CHAPTER 6

PHILOSOPHY AND ETHICS IN ZOROASTRIANISM

Zoroastrianism, like many religions, provides its followers with a philosophy, or guidelines by which to live. A deeply ethical religion, it leads them to make moral choices. Zarathustra's great vision for humankind was to see people as capable of rational thought and fundamentally ethical—that is, able to make right decisions about how they live their lives. For a Zoroastrian the most important religious duty is to lead a moral life.

In Zarathustra's view life is a series of choices between good and evil. He urged his followers to choose goodness. Zoroastrians are taught to strive always to follow the path of Asha, or Truth. To be Zoroastrian is to respect and honor such virtues as truth, kindness, humility, compassion, gratitude, love of family and friends, respect for others and for the community, respect for the environment, kindness to animals, hard work, hospitality, and generosity. These are the Good Thoughts, Good Words, and Good Deeds of Zoroastrianism.

A Zoroastrian priest in front of a modern fire temple in Isfahan, Iran. There is a long tradition of Zoroastrianism in Isfahan, and outside the city in Najafabad high on a hilltop are the remains of a Sassanian-era fire temple.

FOLLOWING THE AMESHA SPENTAS

The Amesha Spentas provide a framework for living the good life that Zarathustra described. They are aspects of Ahura Mazda himself, which later became personified as spirits or angels. By focusing on the virtues represented by the Amesha Spentas, humans may acquire these virtues themselves. The Amesha Spentas thus provide a framework for Zoroastrian life.

ASHA, THE PATH OF TRUTH

Asha is a Gathic word and difficult to translate. The closest translation in English is "truth" and "righteousness," but Asha means more than that. It carries with it the idea of perfection. Asha is truth, wisdom, righteousness, justice, and progress in one ideal. In Zoroastrian belief, there is no higher ideal than Asha. The perfect world of Ahura Mazda is organized according to Asha, the ideal Truth. Zoroastrians try to follow the path of Asha in their lives.

Of all the principles laid down in the Gathas by Zarathustra, Asha is perhaps the most important. Zarathustra mentions it more than any other principle, and he obviously considered it essential to the practice of Zoroastrianism. He says, "For as long as I am able, and have any strength, I shall pursue the Truth [Asha]." (Ys. 28.4) The importance of Asha goes beyond the Gathas. The Ashem Vohu, which is considered the most basic prayer of Zoroastrianism, praises Asha above all things.

Zoroastrians try to pursue and live according to the Truth in their lives but this has never been easy. There may be many truths, although what someone believes is not necessarily true, no matter how sincerely he or she believes it. There are different kinds of truth—for example, spiritual truth and scientific truth. Truth is difficult to know. Moreover, people are

Pursuing the Truth

The entire Yasna, the part of the Avesta that contains the main liturgy and prayers of Zoroastrianism, ends, "There is but one path, that of Asha; all other paths are false paths." Therefore, in order to be Zoroastrian, men and women must practice the principle of Asha in their daily lives. That means that they must try sincerely to pursue the Truth and to live according to it.

limited in their ability to know it by their human viewpoint.

Zoroastrians know that they may pursue Asha for a lifetime and never fully know it. However they must never stop trying to learn it and act according to it. This means constantly searching, constantly learning, constantly questioning, and constantly listening—to other Zoroastrians, to their own conscience, to the words of Zarathustra.

THE GOOD MIND

To help people know and follow the path of Asha, Ahura Mazda has given them Vohu Mana, the Good Mind. Like Asha, this is an aspect of Ahura Mazda that people may aspire to cultivate in their own lives. From the Good Mind of Zoroastrianism come Good Thoughts, and from Good Thoughts follow Good Words and Good Deeds. The Good Mind helps people to choose what is true and valuable in life.

FIGHTING EVIL: A LIFELONG PROCESS

People are not born with Vohu Mana. Indeed learning to be in touch with the Good Mind is a lifelong process. The Good Mind develops through thoughtful study and through being mindful of and practicing goodness. To be always truthful, kind, cheerful, and faithful is a demanding discipline, although it grows easier with practice. There is always temptation toward evil. People must work at not abusing such things as alcohol and sexuality, at being humble and avoiding self-centeredness, at not giving in to laziness and negativity.

In Zoroastrianism it is not enough to refrain from doing evil just because one fears punishment. Evil thoughts are evil. To think evil is to take a step toward doing it. Zoroastrians try always to

REJECTING EVIL

In their *navjote* (initiation) and in their basic daily prayers Zoroastrians repeat their decision to choose Zoroastrianism and to reject evil.

Fravarane Mazdayasno Zarathushtrish vidaevo Ahura-tksesho . . . frame mrute, atha rahtush ashat chit hacha ra ashava . . .

I forthrightly choose the Mazdayasni Zoroastrian religion, opposed to *daevas* [false gods], which follows the Law of Ahura . . . Just as we choose to worship God, so do we choose to venerate the Prophet on account of his holiness.

turn their minds toward righteousness and goodness. They must continually ask themselves, "What is good?" and "What is true?" Moreover, it is not enough to be good oneself if one tolerates evil and ignorance in society or in others. It is necessary to actively fight evil wherever one finds it.

CHOOSING TRUTH AND GOODNESS

The human capacity to think carries with it the responsibility to use the product of thought to make right choices. Zoroastrians choose truth and goodness through their free will. This gift of Ahura Mazda enables them to decide whether they will follow the path of goodness and righteousness or act in ways that are ignorant, sinful, and evil. No one is there to guide them but the goodness that they cultivate within themselves. There is no personal savior, as in Christianity, and no amount of faith will save someone who has chosen the evil path. Zoroastrians must

A *faravahar* symbol above the doorway to a Zoroastrian temple. The symbol reminds people of the purpose of their lives, which is pursuing spiritual progress.

choose right because it is right and for no other reason. Choice is deeply important in Zoroastrianism: At their *navjote*, their initiation ceremony, and in daily prayers ever after, Zoroastrians affirm that they have chosen their religion and to follow the preachings of the prophet Zarathustra.

ARMAITY

Spenta Armaity is the spirit of Generosity and Love. It is the aspect of Ahura Mazda that inspires people to reach out to others. The world is not just spiritual and physical but also social. It is organized into families, associations, workplaces, churches, towns and cities, nations. People have to learn to get along. This does not imply weakness, because Zoroastrians are quick to fight for what they believe to be right. However they try to work through persuasion and example, not force.

There are evils in the social world such as hunger, poverty, warfare, and strife. It is through Armaity that people commit

themselves to love, to help the poor, to work for peace. The spirit of Armaity helps people to perform the acts of charity and kindness that will eventually bring about Ahura Mazda's perfect world.

KHSHATHRA VAIRYA: JUST DOMINION

People who make their own lives rich and pure through following good thoughts, good words, and good deeds find the power of Ahura Mazda within themselves. Khshathra Vairya is not leadership by worldly might but by moral force. Those who acquire it are leaders within their families, within their communities, and out in the world as they work to create a better society. The potential for developing this aspect of Ahura Mazda is within everyone, but achieving the power conferred by Ahura Mazda may take a lifetime.

DUALISM

Zoroastrianism is sometimes described as being based on *dualism*. This is the belief that good and evil are two equal and opposing forces that balance the universe. Zarathustra himself introduced the notion of opposing forces, Truth and the Lie, in the Gathas. In referring to these forces, he used the word *mainyu*, which can mean both "spirit" and "mentality." He called them "twins" (Ys. 30) and said that they "never agree."

Zoroastrians have often debated just what Zarathustra meant when he described these forces. Were they both the creations of Ahura Mazda? Did they already exist in the universe before creation? Or do they exist only within the human heart and mind? The Gathas do not really say. Did Zarathustra mean spirits of the sort to which the human mind can give shape and character? Or was he creating a metaphor about human mentalities, the spirit within? Zoroastrians and historians cannot agree on the interpretation.

GOOD AND EVIL IN ZOROASTRIAN BELIEF

The idea of dualism is the way Zarathustra answered the question that has plagued believers of many religions throughout history. How can the existence of evil in the world be explained? Why doesn't a good and all-powerful God simply do away with evil, ignorance, and injustice?

FRAVASHIS—GUARDIAN SPIRITS

According to Zoroastrian belief Ahura Mazda created the world in two stages. The first was the spiritual, or Menog, stage. Ahura Mazda created the *fravashis* (guardian spirits) of all living things. All things,

It was only in the 18th century that the first portraits of
Zarathustra appeared.

including human life, had no physical form. Everything was pure and without evil. Ahura Mazda asked the *fravashis* if he should give them physical form. He warned that if he did so they would no longer be perfect. Evil would enter the creation. If it did so they would have to fight a long and hard battle to defeat it. The *fravashis*, however, wanted physical bodies. With physical form they would be free to act rather than remain forever in a state of inaction. In return for physical being they would fight Evil.

Ahura Mazda brought the physical, or Getig, world into being. As he had warned, with it came evil in the form of Angra

THE AMESHA SPENTAS

In the history of Zoroastrianism scholars have tended to see Angra Mainyu, or Ahriman, the Spirit of the Lie, as a universal force and cast him as the leader of the forces of evil. This way of looking at the two forces is called *cosmic dualism*. Later thinkers interpret the Gathas as saying that evil is the product of the choices people make in their lives. This view is called *ethical dualism*. Although these two views differ they are not so very far apart. Both agree that good and evil exist and that evil must be conquered.

Name	Meaning	Creation Protected	How Represented in Ritual
Spenta Mainyu	Holy spirit	humankind	the priest
Vohu Mana	Good Mind	animals	milk
Asha	Best righteousness	fire	ritual flame
Armaity	Holy devotion	earth	holy space
Khshathra Vairya	Wise dominion	sky	stone mortar and pestle
Haurvatat	Wholeness	water	consecrated water
Ameretat	Immortality	plants	*haoma* and other plants, flowers

Mainyu, or Ahriman, who would bring imperfection, sin, evil, and death into the world. Ahura Mazda then set the holy spirit, Spenta Mainyu, the Truth, to guide the *fravashis* and to lead the battle against Angra Mainyu, the Lie.

GUMEZISHN

With the twin spirits, Truth and the Lie, the world entered a stage called Gumezishn, the Mixture. This is the stage in which people live today. Good and Bad, Truth and The Lie, both exist in the universe. These two can never agree and so they must fight each other for the souls of humankind. Humans must fight evil in their hearts and minds. This they do with the help of Spenta Mainyu, the holy spirit of Ahura Mazda, and the Beneficent Immortals.

By living ethical lives and following the path of Asha people participate in the battle against Ahriman. Their good actions help to bring about the destruction of evil. Toward the end of this Gumezishn stage, three saviors will be born one thousand years apart. They will lead the righteous in the final battle against evil.

Doorway to the entrance of a Zoroastrian temple in Isfahan, Iran. The doors are engraved with *fravashis*, guardian figures.

SAOSHYANTS: SAVIORS

The term *saoshyant* (savior) was applied to Zarathustra's followers because he believed that the apocalypse was near. There was urgency in his efforts to gather as many followers as he could to fight and conquer the hostile spirit and usher in the *Frashokereti*, the renewal at the end of the world. He pleaded, "May we be those who make existence brilliant." When the apocalypse did

AHURA MAZDA KHODAE

From one of the basic daily prayers of Zoroastrianism:

Ahuramazda Khodae, Ahreman. Awadashan, dur awazdashtar zad shekashteh bad! Ahreman, devan, darujan, jaduan, darvandan, kikan, karafan, sastaran, gunehgaran, ashmogam, darvandan, dushmana frian Zad shekashteh bad; dush-padshahan awadashan bad . . .

Ahuramazda Kohdae, az hama gunah patet pashemanum, az harvastin dushmata, duzukhta, duzhvarshta, mem pa geti manid oem goft, oem kard, oem jast, oem bun bud ested. Az an gunah, manashni, gavashni, kunashni, tani ravani, geti minoani, okhe awaksh pasheman pa se gavashni pa patet hom. Khshnaothra Ahurae Mazdao! Taroidite Anghrahe Mainyeush! Haithya varshtam huat vasna ferashotemem. Staomi Ashem.

Ahura Mazda is the self-created master. May the evil mind be vanquished and removed far from us. May it be frustrated and defeated. May the evil mentality, the wicked persons, the liars, the deceivers, those who have left the right path, the willfully blind, the willfully deaf, the tyrants, the sinners, the distorters of truth, the persons who have strayed from the path of God, the evil minded, may they all be frustrated and may the evil minded be defeated and removed far from us . . .

Ahura Mazda is our lord. From all my sins I repent. I turn back from every evil thought, every evil word, and every evil deed, which in this world I may have thought, I may have uttered, I may have committed, or which in any way proceeded from me or originated from me. From all such sins of thoughts, words, and deeds, pertaining either to my body or my soul, pertaining either to this world or the spiritual world, I do turn back having conscientiously sought forgiveness by expressing repentance three times over for it. The glory be unto Ahura Mazda! Let there be contempt for the evil mind! Such is the uppermost wish of those who are virtuous in their actions. I praise Truth.

(In Framroz Rustomjee, *Daily Prayers of the Zoroastrians*, 1959.)

not come immediately, the *saoshyant* was no longer viewed as a general portrait of all those who worked toward "the end." The *saoshyant* was transformed into a particular figure who would bring about "the end."

Eventually the vision of the *saoshyant* focused on three successive *saoshyants* separated by thousands of years. They would usher in eras of peace after the forces of evil seemed to prevail. The appearance of the first of these saviors would mark the decline of the trend toward evil and a reversal to a time of justice, peace, and piety.

In time all people die but their *fravashis* and their souls are immortal. Where their souls exist in the afterlife reflects the choices they made during life. All their thoughts, words, and deeds in their lifetime become part of their soul. Those who have sincerely followed the path of Asha may pass confidently into the Abode of Songs, or heaven. The others fall into the abyss of hell.

In Zoroastrian thought, however, hell is not permanent. It exists only until, as will surely happen, good overcomes evil. Then the dead will rise, purified and redeemed. Even Ahriman will repent and return to the worship of Ahura Mazda.

Frashogard

All Zoroastrians work through their good deeds and through living moral and ethical lives to a time when good will overcome evil. This is called Frashogard or Frashokereti, which means "renewal" or "freshening." The physical and spiritual worlds will be united in a perfect stage of the world before creation of the physical world, called Menog. All creation will exist in this stage forever in a state of perfection.

CHAPTER 7

RITUALS AND RITES OF PASSAGE

L ike most religions, Zoroastrianism has many meaningful rituals. The origins of these, such as the Yasna, stretch back into prehistory. They probably come from Iranian religious custom in the time before Zarathustra. In Zoroastrianism priests perform the religion's highly prescribed rituals in consecrated temples at regular intervals throughout the day. These rituals are closed to all but confirmed members of the faith who are in a state of ritual purity. Those who qualify may attend, although there is no requirement to do so. The basic rituals consist of caring for the consecrated fire; performing the Yasna rituals; and purifying those who have come in contact with pollution. The priests may also offer prayers and special rituals for individuals who request them.

Except for the Vendidad, which is read aloud by a priest, the priests memorize all the rituals. The language of the ritual is Avestan, which is believed to be especially pleasing to the ear of Ahura Mazda. Traditionally the basic ritual of the Yasna has been the *haoma* ritual, in which priests ritually extract juice from the *haoma* plant as an offering.

Parsi priests lead boys in the *navjote,* the tying of the sacred thread—*kusti*—around the body.

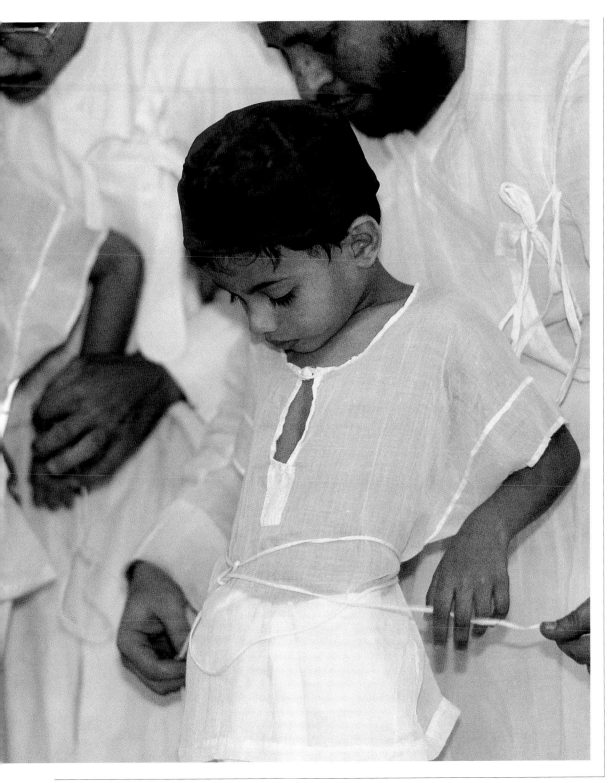

KEEPING THE SACRED FIRE

Zoroastrian tradition says that the great fires of their religion have been burning since prehistory. The first fire is said to have been brought from heaven on the back of the mythical ox Srishok to be the guide and protector of humankind for all time. Fire represents the spiritual rule of light over darkness and is the sacred symbol of Ahura Mazda.

Behram fire is the most powerful of all temple fires. It protects against the powers of darkness and does battle with the Lie. In the *atash behram* the fire rests on a platform over which is a crown that represents its power. The Behram fire is made up of fires gathered from 16 different sources specified in the Avesta. One source must be fire ignited by lightning, which comes directly from Ahura Mazda; others are consecrated fires from other professions and places where fire is used, such as the bakers, the dyers, the goldsmiths, the potters. The rituals for purifying a fire are performed 1,128 times, a process that takes a year. The most sacred fires of Zoroastrianism reside in consecrated temples in Iran and India. They have been burning continuously for centuries. The first fire in India was consecrated by ritual implements that were carried overland from Iran. Later on the fires in India were consecrated in India itself.

The Highest Rituals

The highest rituals of Zoroastrianism may be carried out only in the presence of consecrated fire, which is kept only in a fire temple built with specially consecrated tools and consecrated with a series of rituals. In North America and other countries around the world there is no consecrated temple or consecrated fire. People send their special prayer requests to the high priests in India or Iran, where the holiest of ceremonies are celebrated.

THE *BOI* CEREMONY

The ceremony that accompanies the regular tending of the fire five times a day is called *boi-machi.* The fire is usually fed with sandalwood, which has a sweet odor when burned; worshippers may purchase it at the temple and donate it as an offering. In an *atash behram,* the highest grade of fire temple, it is tended by white-gloved priests who have undergone the most rigorous purification.

The priest prays the appropriate prayers and then places over the fire six pieces of

THE ZOROASTRIAN CALENDARS

The Zoroastrians of Persia had a calendar of 12 30-day months, or 360 days. They added five special "Gatha Days" to bring the calendar closer to the actual 365-day year. Instead of adding a day every four years to account for the extra one-quarter day each year, as is done in today's Western Gregorian calendar, they added a month every 120 years to bring the months back into line with the seasons. At some point, however, they stopped adding the extra month. Their calendar was called *Qadmi* or *Kadmi*.

The Parsis took the Persian calendar to India with them. They continued to add the extra month, so their calendar came to differ from the Qadmi calendar. In 1720 a priest visiting from Iran noticed that the Iranians and the Parsis were using different calendars. Some returned to the Qadmi calendar used by the Iranians. Others stayed with their calendar, called Shenshai.

To try to reconcile the two, a scholar recommended using a more modern calendar of 365¼ days. That way the spring equinox (the date when night and day are the same length) always falls on March 21. Those who adopted this calendar called it Fasli for "following the seasons."

As a result there are three different Zoroastrian calendars, and different groups of Zoroastrians celebrate their gahambars (holy festivals) at different times of the year. On the Fasli calendar Navruz (Zoroastrian New Year's) always falls on March 21, but on the Qadmi or Shenshai calendars it may fall in July or August.

sandalwood (or other dry wood in the shape of a throne), frankincense, and herbs, which fumigate and give out a pleasant smell. Then the wood is placed in the fire urn, or *afargan*. In the highest fire temple the priest, carrying a metal ladle, then circles the fire, stopping eight times to repeat a prayer in Avestan, which means the following:

O Ahura Mazda, we praise Thee through Thy visible
symbol, the fire. We praise Thee by our offering of
Good thoughts, words, and deeds.
(In The Zoroastrian Society of Greater New York, *The Good Life*.)

The priest then strikes a bell nine times, symbolically calling the holy spirit to be present in the room. After the ceremony the priest uses the ladle to give ash from the fire to any worshippers who are present.

The Zoroastrian priesthood has traditionally been hereditary in the male line, although now in Iran men may qualify through study. The duties of priests include reciting the liturgy in the temples and in the homes of members of the community, saying prayers for the dead, and conducting weddings, *navjotes* (initiation ceremonies), and *jashans* (rituals of memorial and thanksgiving). Zoroastrian priests are known as *mobeds*; in India they are called dasturs. There are several levels in the priestly hierarchy. The highest grade of priest is known as a *mobed e mobedan.* *Mobedyars* are priests in training.

TRAINING AND ORDINATION

In India priestly training usually begins immediately after *navjote* when children are about seven years old. It requires memorizing the basic scriptures and liturgy, after which they have to undergo a ceremony that requires a series of purification rituals. The basic liturgy, the Yasna, is always recited in Avestan, so memorization is by heart. The candidate spends a period of nine days in retreat and undergoes a second purification ritual. Then he is dressed in white, the color of purity, and ordained by a senior *mobed.* After the ritual he recites the Yasna. Over the following days he recites other liturgies, earning the right to be called *ervad,* a title for a Zoroastrian priest. The candidate may

Zoroastrian priests—*mobeds*—study together at a religious college in Iran.

A consecrated fire continually burns in the *afragan,* the urn
holding the fire, in the Zoroastrian temple in London. Fire is
the symbol of Ahura Mazda, capturing the brilliance of the
sun and the heavenly bodies. It also captures
the energy of Truth.

perform basic ceremonies, including the *navjote* and wedding ceremonies, although he may not celebrate high rituals, including the Yasna. Many young men stop at this level and go into other professions.

MASTERY OF THE RITUALS

If he is to continue, the young priest then spends the next two to three years learning additional scriptures before undergoing further purification rituals and a higher initiation called the *maratab*. The young priest will then become a full *mobed*. When he has demonstrated a mastery of all the rituals he is qualified to perform any Zoroastrian ceremony. As a rule candidates for the priesthood learn the rituals by memorization and practice. They are not expected to learn Avestan and Pahlavi, although they may take lessons in the meaning of the rituals through translation. If they attend college later they may study the languages of Zoroastrianism at that time.

The examination for the priesthood in Iran is similar but candidates are tested more intensively on their knowledge and understanding of the religion, and there is only one grade of priest. The new *mobed* practices with others for a year, after which he is on his own.

THE HOLY DAYS OF ZOROASTRIANISM

Zoroastrians do not gather weekly for regular worship services. Instead they recite the basic daily prayers five times daily, either alone, in informal groups, or as a family. They do, however, have holidays or festivals during which they join together for worship and celebration.

There are seven great Zoroastrian festivals each year. Ancient in origin, they are linked to the Iranian agricultural year and to the seven physical creations for which the Amesha Spentas are responsible. In the *atash behrams* priests recite the holy

Gahambar

Gahambar or "proper season" is the term for six of the seven holy days instituted by Zarathustra to honor Ahura Mazda and the Amesha Spentas. The seventh holy day is Navruz, the New Year festival.

day's special liturgy. People participate in the *jashan,* or thanksgiving and memorial ceremony, and follow the special custom of the day, which may be merrymaking, putting on new clothes, or visiting the fire temple.

The six Zoroastrian *gahambars* (festivals) are:

Maidhyoizarem (Midspring)
Maidhyoishem (Midsummer)
Paitshahem (Harvest)
Ayathrem (Bringing in Cattle)
Maidhyairem (Midwinter)
Hamaspathmaedem Muktad (All Souls)

The seventh and highest festival is Navruz, the New Year. The festival celebrates the creation of fire and the Beneficent Immortal Asha Vahista, or Highest Truth. It is thus the most sacred and joyous of all Zoroastrian holy days. It is held in the spring, just after the sixth *gahambar,* and so represents the renewal of life that spring symbolizes. It also represents the new order to come with Frashogard, world renewal. On Navruz people exchange presents, put on new clothes, settle any outstanding arguments, and visit their fire temple to reaffirm their faith. Zoroastrians celebrate *gahambars* as part of their religious duty. They believe that such times of community joy and harmony provide a glimpse of the spiritual world.

Community Giving

The holy days are times when the entire community, both rich and poor, comes together to share a feast to which everyone contributes according to their ability. In ancient times a ruler might bring barrels of wine and whole roasted animals, and a poor man bring a single onion, but all contributed to the joy and merriment of the occasion.

JASHAN: THE THANKSGIVING AND MEMORIAL CEREMONY

Jashan is a ceremony for thanksgiving and memorializing. It is performed during the *gahambars* and Navruz but it may be performed at any time that people want to express gratitude and happiness, as for a wedding, a *navjote,* a housewarming, or the

SEVEN HOLY DAYS OF ZOROASTRIANISM

The *Gahambars*

English Name	Amesha Spenta	Associated Creation	Time of Year*
Midspring	Khshathra	sky	April/May
Midsummer	Haurvatat	water	June/July
Bringing in Corn	Spenta Armaity	earth	September
Homecoming	Ameratat	plants	October
Midwinter	Vohu Mana	cattle	January
All Souls	Spenta Mainyu/ Ahura Mazda	humankind	March
New Year (Navruz)	Asha Vahista	fire	March

*These are the approximate times according to the ancient and present Zoroastrian Fasli calendar.

dedication of a new fire temple. Individuals may also sponsor a *jashan* for a celebration or in memory of someone who has died.

REMEMBRANCE AND CELEBRATION

During the *jashan* the priests sit on the floor on either side of a cloth that contains an *afargan,* or fire urn, a tray of sandalwood and incense for feeding the fire, and a tray of offerings of flowers, fruit, milk, bread, and frequently wine. They begin by lighting the fire and offering prayers to consecrate it. They then remember the departed souls of the faithful, starting with Zarathustra and Zoroastrian heroes. They first repeat prayers related to the person or event being celebrated or remembered. In the next part of the *jashan* the flowers on

The Spiritual and Physical Worlds

The *jashan* requires at least two priests, who take the parts of the *zaotar* (speaker) and the *raspi* (assistant), but often four participate. The ceremony represents a dialogue between the spiritual and the physical worlds, symbolically linking the two. It invites Ahura Mazda, the Amesha Spentas, the *yazatas,* and the *fravashis* and souls of the dead to join in.

At the Navruz or New Year celebrations, some families have a tradition of placing something sweet in a safe place outside the house overnight. On the first morning of Navruz, the first person awake brings the sweets into the house to symbolize the coming of good fortune in the year ahead.

the tray before them are exchanged during the recitation of a prayer. The exchange of flowers symbolizes the journey of the *fravashis* from heaven to the earthly world and back. They repeat the yatha ahu vairyo and Ashem vohu prayers and the prayers of thanksgiving. The priest calls on the spiritual world to bless the worshippers, reciting a special prayer, the Afringan, for those who sponsored the *jashan*. The ceremony is then at an end.

The ceremony is an expression of happiness: gratitude for past blessings and joy in the good things in the present and future. The *jashan* may be a private affair or accompanied by a feast in which all members of the community participate.

THANKSGIVING DAYS

Zoroastrians celebrate other thanksgiving days as well. These include the dates of the Prophet's birth and death and days that recall the *yazatas*, such as the divinity of Rain and Fertility, the divinity of Water, and Mithra, the divinity of Sun and Justice. They also celebrate the five Gatha days at the end of the year by remembering the *fravashis* of those who have died and by giving thanks for those in the present world whom they love and care for.

> ### FROM THE KUSTI PRAYERS
>
> *I profess myself a Mazda worshipper and follower of Zarathustra, I pledge myself to the well-thought thought . . . to the well-spoken word . . . to the well-acted act . . . Ohrmazd is Lord! Ahriman he keeps at bay . . .*
>
> *May Ahriman be struck and defeated, with devs and drujs, sorcerers and sinners, enemies and witches. May they all be struck and defeated . . .*
>
> *O Ohrmazd, Lord! I am contrite for all sins and I desist from them all, from all bad thoughts, bad words and bad acts which I have thought, spoken, or done in the world, or which have happened through me, or have originated with me. For those sins . . .*
>
> *I am contrite, I renounce them . . . with Satisfaction for Ahura Mazda, scorn for Angra Mainyu! . . . I praise Asha (righteousness).*
>
> (In Mary Boyce, *Textual Sources for the Study of Zoroastrianism*, 1984.)

NAVJOTE

The ceremony in which young people are initiated into Zoroastrianism is known as *navjote*. Among Iranian Zoroastrians the age for *navjote* or, as it is called there, *sudre-pushti*, has traditionally been 15. Parsi Zoroastrians perform it at an earlier age, usually seven or nine, but no later than 11.

Training in the way of faith, which begins in babyhood, is the responsibility of the parents. With the *navjote* young people take on the responsibility for their own lives by choosing good over evil. From that time on their parents are no longer responsible for their actions. The *navjote* is the same for both boys and girls.

At the *navjote* the initiate receives the symbols of the religion. These are the *sudreh* and the *kusti*. The *sudreh* is a white muslin garment ceremonially made, which devout Zoroastrians wear as an undergarment. It symbolizes purity. The *kusti* is a cord that is wrapped around the body. It is woven from lamb's wool and symbolizes Vohu Mana, the Good Mind. Besides being a reminder that the wearer is bound to the Good Religion, the *kusti* plays an important part in Zoroastrian daily prayer and ritual.

CLEANSING THE BODY AND SOUL

The initiate comes to the *navjote* freshly bathed. Before the ceremony begins the young person recites special prayers, including the Kusti prayers that are part of daily worship. He or she is then asked to sip a consecrated liquid. Traditionally this has been *nirang,* bull's urine that has been ritually prepared, although pomegranate juice is often used today. The drink ritually cleanses the body and soul within. Then the initiate recites a series of prayers, including the Ashem Vohu, the "Principle of Righteousness," in a prescribed order. He or she then goes for a ritual bath, or *nahan*. These actions symbolize inner and outer purification.

ACCEPTING THE *SUDREH* AND TYING THE *KUSTI*

After the *nahan* the initiate returns to the room where the ceremony will be held, dressed entirely in white and wearing the white cap that Zoroastrians always wear during prayer. The officiating priest recites the Patet, or "repentance," prayer, which represents

After receiving the *sudreh* and *kusti,* as a necessary part of the *navjote* ritual, the initiate recites a declaration of his or her faith in Ahura Mazda. The priest—or priests, if more than one is attending—offers a final blessing, completing the ceremony. The young person is now a full member of the Zoroastrian faith.

a turning away from sin. After that the initiate and the priest stand facing each other, holding the *sudreh* together. Together they recite the Din No Kalmo, or "Declaration of Faith." Next the priest puts the *sudreh* on the initiate. In taking the *sudreh* the initiate symbolically accepts the responsibility of working for good and helping to bring about the final renovation of the world.

The priest then stands behind the initiate and ties on the *kusti* according to prescribed ritual, while the two pray aloud together. The *kusti* is circled around the initiate's waist three times and knotted four times. The three circles around the waist represent Good Thoughts, Good Words, and Good Deeds. The exact symbolic meaning of the knots is not known, but one explanation is that the first represents one God, the second that Zoroastrianism is the word of God, the third that Zarathustra is the Prophet of God, and the fourth is a reminder that the wearer is bound to the religion forever. Zoroastrians are to wear the *kusti* at all times, tying and untying it and reciting the basic prayers and according to tradition on getting up, after using the bathroom, before daily prayers, after a bath, and before meals.

RITUAL AND BELIEF IN ZOROASTRIANISM

Ritual, whether the high ritual of the *atash behram,* the *navjote,* or the *jashan* gathering in a community hall, is an important part of Zoroastrianism. The rituals of Zoroastrianism carry the Zoroastrian believer from birth to death, marking the important rites of passage and times of joy and sorrow, creating occasions for celebration and unity. In the ancient Zoroastrian rituals and prayers are all of the history of the faith and the poetry of the Gathas. The unbroken tradition of Zoroastrian ritual has helped to keep the religion strong and alive through more than 3,000 years.

WEDDINGS

Zoroastrians are expected to marry and produce children, the only way in which Zoroastrianism can grow and prosper. The participants all wear white, the color worn by Zoroastrians on religious occasions. Traditionally Zoroastrian weddings are held at home, although hotels and other meeting places may be used. The groom often enters in a procession of musicians and guests led by a priest. At least two priests lead the ceremony. The couple sits next to each other with witnesses, usually members of each family, behind them. Like all Zoroastrian ceremonies the wedding takes place in the presence of a fire.

The ceremony begins with a blessing. The senior priest expresses the hope that the couple will have long lives, lasting love, health and strength, and be blessed with children and grandchildren. The priest then asks the witnesses if they agree to the union and, when the answer is yes, asks the couple if they have agreed "with a righteous mind" to be married until the end of their lives. Each replies individually, "We have agreed." The ceremony recalls the wedding of Pouruchista and Jamaspa, during which Zarathustra asked his daughter if she freely agreed to the marriage.

Priests and witnesses may pass a long string around the couple, symbolically binding them together, and then offer prayers and blessings. The couple are showered with rice, symbolic of prosperity and joy.

Airyema Ishyo

Airyema is the *yazata*, or spirit, of friendship and of healing. The prayer, written in Avestan, is recited especially at weddings.

May longed-for Airyaman come to the support of the men and women of Zarathustra, to the support of good purpose. The Inner Self which earns the reward to be chosen, for it I ask the longed-for recompense of truth, which Lord Mazda will have in mind.

(In Mary Boyce, *Textual Sources for the Study of Zoroastrianism*, 1984.)

FUNERALS

In Zoroastrian tradition death represents the strongest form of ritual impurity or pollution. Therefore Zoroastrians have strict rituals associated with death and dying. These rituals begin even before death. If a person is known to be dying family members bring a fire into the room to drive away evil.

According to Zoroastrian belief the evil spirit of decay rushes into the body within three hours after death. Because of the extreme pollution of death no one may touch the dead except special "corpse bearers," who are specially trained and who undergo special purification rituals after their work is done. Anyone else who touches the body must undergo ritual purification, or *nahan*. All of the rituals surrounding death stress that the living should avoid the pollution of death.

DEPARTURE OF THE SOUL

The corpse bearers ritually wash the body and dress it in a clean *sudreh* and *kusti*. The body is shrouded with only the face uncovered. They place the body on a stone slab and mark an area around

A *dakhma,* or tower of silence, the traditional place of disposal of the dead, stands on an Iranian hilltop outside the town of Yazd. In the foreground are traditional wind towers which harness the wind to provide ventilation and cool air in homes and buildings.

INSIDE A TOWER OF SILENCE

Plan of a *dakhma,* or tower of silence. The structure is open to the sky. Dead bodies are placed on stone slabs: men on the outer ring, women in the middle, and children in the inner ring. Drains carry any matter not consumed by vultures away to a central well, which is sprinkled with acid from time to time for sanitation. Any remaining fragments are carried by drains to underground wells, where they return gradually to the earth.

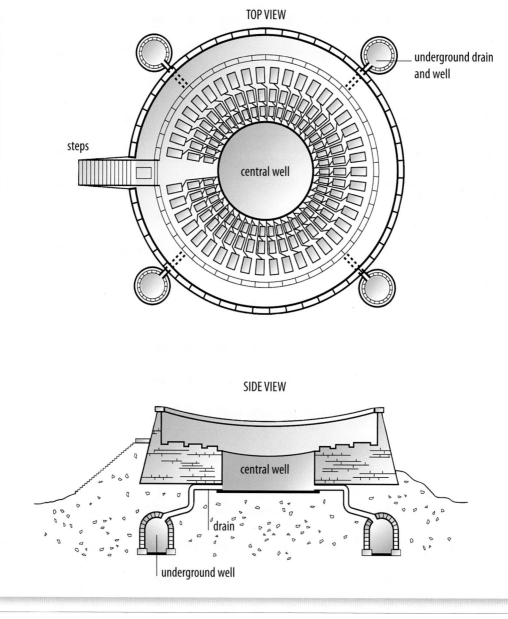

TOP VIEW

underground drain and well

steps

central well

SIDE VIEW

central well

drain

underground well

the body into which the priests and family may not step. Fire fed with sandalwood and frankincense is kept burning beside the body to keep evil spirits away. A priest then comes and prays in Avestan. The priest is joined by at least one other for the *geh sarna* ceremony, in which they recite the first Gatha of Zarathustra. The *geh sarna* ceremony signals the departure of the soul from the body. After the ceremony the body is no longer connected to the soul and may be disposed of.

SAGDID CEREMONY

The members of the household say their goodbyes by looking on the body of the dead person, but without touching it. The corpse bearers then carry it out of the house on a metal bier (metal and stone do not absorb pollution, as wood does). Outside, the body is placed on a stone slab and a dog is brought to look on the face of the dead person, a ceremony known as *sagdid*. The dog both verifies death and drives away evil. Then the corpse bearers, followed by two priests and the mourners, carry the body to its final destination.

TOWERS OF SILENCE

In Zoroastrianism, since death is the ultimate victory of Ahriman over life, a dead body represents a state of extreme pollution. It should not be allowed, therefore, to pollute the sacred elements: fire, water, air, or earth. The traditional way of disposing of a corpse in India and Iran has been the *dakhma*, or tower of silence. This is a circular stone building open at the top, usually set on a barren hill. The inside is arranged in three circles. The outer circle is for men, the middle for women, and the inner circle for children.

Only corpse handlers may enter the building. They carry the body to the building, pause outside for mourners to say their last goodbyes, and then take the body inside and place it on a stone slab, where it is left to be devoured by vultures. The mourners withdraw to pray and then return home, where they pray and ritually bathe to cleanse themselves of the pollution of death.

The use of bull's urine, or *nirang,* in Zoroastrian purification ritual has ancient roots. In prehistoric times, and in some traditional religions today, sickness and death were believed to be caused by evil spirits. Priests and shamans were often the keepers of medical lore as well as religious ritual.

The ancients knew that urine had healing properties—a bit of medical knowledge that would not be fully understood by modern science until the 18th century. Thousands of years before modern antiseptics urine could be used to cleanse a wound and prevent infection. From this it was only a short step to its being used in ritual as a purifying agent. It was followed by washing in water.

In general only those who needed to be in a state of high ritual purity, such as priests, or who required cleansing after coming into contact with extreme pollution, such as death, underwent purification rituals with *nirang,* which is also called *gomez,* or *taro* (unconsecrated bull's urine). It is rarely if ever used today.

Throughout the following year the family offers appropriate prayers for the dead.

In recent times Zoroastrians have had to find other methods of disposing of their dead. *Dakhmas* are now in use mainly in parts of western India, where the custom was established before the 1800s. The most traditional Zoroastrians around the world may return their dead to their home country, where they can be placed in a *dakhma.* Newer Parsi communities in India now have burial grounds and Iranian Zoroastrians now use burial as well. Zoroastrians in other parts of the world may also use modern methods of cremation. Today's Zoroastrians reason that the prayers and rituals surrounding death are more important than the disposal of the body, so the least polluting method is considered appropriate.

PRAYERS FOR THE DEAD

At dawn on the third day after death the soul goes to meet the three judges, Mithra, Sraosha, and Rashnu. They judge the soul on its actions in life. It then passes on to the Chinvat Bridge, the Bridge of the Separator. There it meets its *daena,* the guide who will take it across. She represents the person's conscience in life. If that life has been righteous *daena* is beautiful beyond all imagining and is accompanied by a sweet-smelling breeze. If the life has been one of ignorance and evil the guide is an ugly hag with a foul odor. The two move across the bridge. For the righteous the bridge is wide and flat and leads into eternal joy. For the wicked it becomes narrower and narrower until it is a knife blade, and the wicked soul falls off into the pit of hell.

Illustration from the 19th century of the Towers of Silence, where the dead are laid to be consumed by vultures, at Malabar Hill, Mumbai, India.

During this time priests and the family continue with special prayers for the dead. Mourners may continue to recite the Patet, a prayer of repentance, and other prayers in honor and remembrance of the dead person daily for a month or even longer. Their prayers cannot, however, change the fate of the soul, which has been decided according to the dead person's behavior in life.

Excessive mourning is considered a sin in Zoroastrianism. It does not benefit the dead and it harms the health of the living. Zoroastrianism teaches that the dead have moved on to eternal life and that in the final renovation of the world all the dead will rise. People remember the dead, but their duty as Zoroastrians is to live fully in this world and be happy and optimistic. Feast days always include rituals for the dead, but as an occasion for joy, not sorrow.

CHAPTER 8

ZOROASTRIANISM: FACING THE FUTURE

A generous estimate would admit that there are only about 200,000 Zoroastrians in the world today. Compared with Christians, Muslims, Hindus, and Buddhists this is a very small number. Zoroastrianism is a religion that is local; it is a religion that began in ancient Persia (or modern Iran). Through Muslim persecution it became also a diaspora religion, spreading in 936 C.E. according to the traditional date, to India.

More recently, due to the establishment of an Islamic republic in Iran by the Ayatollah Khomeini in 1979, many more Zoroastrians have left their native land and migrated to Britain, Australia, Canada, and the United States. Zoroastrians therefore are not only small in numbers, but also a people who are dispersed. There are still strong communities of Zoroastrians in Iran and in India, where despite the challenges of modern life and political difficulties, they hold to their traditions and adapt them to contemporary circumstances. Wherever they may be, however, Zoroastrians make efforts to keep their religious communities

Zoroastrian priests performing *jashan* ceremony which invokes certain *fravashis,* guardian spirits, depending on the occasion. During the ceremony, two priests recite scriptures to bring blessings down on the living and those present, or to bring blessings to those who have died and are remembered at the ceremony.

alive and active. Frequently Zoroastrian communities sponsor social and religious events that promote their identity by supporting lectures, adult discussion groups, and circles that study the Gathas. They also run instruction classes to teach the young about their religion and sponsor youth groups to bring together the bright hope of their future.

ZOROASTRIAN YOUTH

Zoroastrianism today has two main strands: traditional Zoroastrianism and updated Zoroastrianism. The former is very much anchored in its Persian and Indian roots. In traditional Zoroastrianism emphasis is placed on the identification of Zoroastrians as members of both a religious community and an ethnic group. This traditionalist view strongly recommends marriage only between Zoroastrians. The future of Zoroastrianism for these people is focused on the offspring of these unions: Zoroastrians beget Zoroastrians. In the vision of the traditional Zoroastrians the young are the only future for the religion.

Updated Zoroastrianism has a different vision of the future. For its proponents Zoroastrianism is a religion, not an ethnic group. They believe that their religious future is not with the young alone but also with converts from outside the ethnic circle. Still, each Zoroastrian group realizes the importance of youth for its future.

Both approaches to the religion make strong efforts to unite their young members through associations. One such association, the Zoroastrian Youth of North America (ZYNA), organizes activities for young people in the United States and Canada who are between the ages of 16 and 35. By means of summer camps and weekend retreats this organization provides opportunities for young Zoroastrians to meet one another and to participate in discussions of their religious traditions. This association is cochaired by young people from Vancouver, British Columbia; New York; and Boston. Another association, under the umbrella

Women prepare bread for a community meal in Iran during Navruz, the Zoroastrian new year celebration.

of Zoroastrian Youth of North America, is the Zoroastrian Student Association at the University of Michigan, which sponsors forums and lectures for graduate and undergraduate students. Zoroastrians pay great attention to the young—from those who are just beginning school all the way up to those who are finishing their professional degrees.

THE FUTURE OF ZOROASTRIANISM

Like many small religious communities such as the Orthodox Jews, Zoroastrians wonder about their survival under modern pressures. The future seems particularly fragile among the Zoroastrians of the diaspora. There is such a limited number of the faithful and they are surrounded by cultures alien to their way of life and by religions that are better known and more affirmed by society. Ritual practices, which are so important for fostering and preserving community and so essential for traditionalists, often become watered down or even neglected in a diaspora world. Important religious reminders, such as the wearing of the *sudreh* and *kusti,* are often set aside (except for ceremonies) because some young believers wish to avoid standing out in a crowd.

Because the priesthood is hereditary and there are so few sons of priests who want to continue in their fathers' footsteps in a world so distant from the world of traditional Zoroastrianism, continuance of worship becomes a problem. Also, Zoroastrian practices of burial are so foreign to those practiced in diaspora lands that it seems totally implausible that such rituals can be followed anywhere outside of Iran and India.

The most sacred rituals—those that take place in an *atash behram*—cannot be transported to diaspora lands, as there is also no consecrated fire outside of Iran and India. The result is that Zoroastrians in the United States, Canada, Australia, and Great Britain are limited to celebrating festivals or having social events, forums, and lectures in *darbe mehrs,* or fire temples. None of these are fundamental Zoroastrian rituals.

Most of the young in the diaspora worlds, then, have had no experience of a sacred ritual and have never entered an *atash beh-*

ram. The consequence of all of this ignorance is that these deeper aspects of their religion have little meaning for them.

Nevertheless there are many efforts to nourish religious faith in spite of these limitations. Many modern Zoroastrians emphasize the ethical character of their religion more than the importance of ritual practices. They view the main teaching of Zarathustra as concerning itself with the discipline of good thoughts, good words, good deeds, and daily prayer.

RELIGIOUS DIFFERENCES

Many tensions arise between traditional and liberal Zoroastrians because they have two very different views of their religion. The first group stresses the importance of the rituals and the limiting conditions of place that surround them. For them the Vendidad, or priestly code, with its ritual prescriptions, is very important. These prescriptions cannot be set aside and the traditional rituals cannot be adapted in any way.

FIRE TEMPLES IN NORTH AMERICA

Darbe mehrs—fire temples—have been established across the continent, starting in 1977.

- Arbab Rustom Guiv Darbe Mehr, New York, 1977
- Mehraban Guiv Darbe Mehr, Toronto, Ontario 1978
- Arbab Rustom Guiv Darbe Mehr, Chicago, 1983
- Arbab Rustom Guiv Darbe Mehr, Vancouver, British Columbia, 1985
- Rustom Guiv Dar-e Mehr, Los Angeles, 1986
- North American Zoroastrian Center, Washington, D.C., 1990
- Zoroastrian Heritage and Cultural Center, Houston, Texas, 1996

LEGACY OF ETHICAL TEACHINGS

Modern Zoroastrians stress the ethical teachings of Zarathustra as his central legacy. For them rituals are not the very essence of Zoroastrianism; and certainly their performance is, in practical terms, impossible outside the ancient sites of Iran and India. Liberal Zoroastrians are therefore willing to set aside the ritual practices for everyday life. Some claim that it is impossible to carry out these ritual practices in modern circumstances. Others set the rituals aside simply because they see no reason to preserve them. For them the Zoroastrian way of life—good thoughts, good words, and good deeds—is what is central to Zoroastrianism. For them ritual-centered religion does not travel well around the world or in modern times. Modern Zoroastrians therefore focus upon Zarathustra's ethical teachings. They would rather meditate upon or discuss one of Zarathustra's Gathas than carry out a purification rite or even join in the chanting of a Gatha.

TRADITIONAL AND LIBERAL VIEWPOINTS

The question for Zoroastrians in today's world seems to be whether or not they can pick and choose any interpretation of the religion of Zarathustra they want to follow. The conservative or traditionalist approach is to argue that one has to accept the whole message—the ethical code *and* the ritual of the Zoroastrian tradition. The liberal or modern interpretation sees the ethical message as the real essence of Zarathustra's religious contribution to the world of modern man. Some effort of accommodation seems necessary for the survival of Zoroastrianism, or a small group of dedicated religious people is going to wear itself out through serious family disputes.

THE QUESTION OF INTERMARRIAGE

Among the most hotly debated issues that splits traditionalist from liberal Zoroastrians is the question of intermarriage. The

A fire being kindled in a Zoroastrian temple. The fire is usually fed with sandalwood which gives a sweet odor when burnt. It can be purchased by worshippers at the temple or they may bring it as offerings.

tradition among Zoroastrians was to marry other Zoroastrians as a way of strengthening and extending the religious and ethnic community. In the strongest traditional community, that of the Parsis in India, it is traditionally forbidden to marry someone of another religion. In their view intermarriage begets religious compromises and discord. To marry someone of another faith is to abandon your own faith. For the Parsi a person who intermarries is traditionally no longer considered a Zoroastrian. The children of such unions are also not considered "full" Zoroastrians; they are forbidden to take part in the highest religious rituals and may not enter the presence of the most sacred fires.

For the traditionalist Zoroastrians the child of a Zoroastrian father may be accepted for *navjote*—the traditional ceremony of confirmation—in the Zoroastrian religion. A child of a Zoroastrian mother would not be accepted. For the liberal Zoroastrians of the diaspora, however, such a distinction between the treatment of children of Zoroastrian fathers and mothers is unfair: So the children of either Zoroastrian parent may be confirmed.

COMMUNITY SURVIVAL

Such rules concerning membership seem quite reasonable when they are seen in terms of community survival. A small community has its best hope of survival in keeping to itself. This can be seen from the stories of other peoples. Many of the Jewish people lost their identity and their biblical roots when the Assyrians captured them. The Assyrians had a policy of sending conquered people into different lands so that they would lose their identity through intermarriage. As a result they would not be unified enough to rebel against their conquerors. A further consideration, however, is that in Persia and in India Zoroastrians had religiously solid and somewhat large Zoroastrian communities where it was quite possible to find a suitable Zoroastrian mate.

PRESERVING THE FAITH IN THE DIASPORA

In the modern world, especially in the world of the diaspora where Zoroastrians are spread throughout many countries in small numbers, these conditions for suitable and favorable marriages with others of the same faith have disappeared. Certainly Zoroastrians make all kinds of efforts to foster connections between young Zoroastrian men and women through associations and social events; even so the odds seem stacked against finding someone with the same beliefs when so few exist who hold them. Permitting intermarriage seems most reasonable under these circumstances. However the concerns that fostered prohibitions against intermarriage continue to surface: If Zoroastrians intermarry will they be able to preserve their religious identity?

Both traditionalist and liberal Zoroastrians recognize the dilemma they face, and though they are divided over how to resolve it, many in both groups have some understanding of the opposing view. They realize that on the one hand, marriage within the religion will be for the good of preserving the religion. They hold as a Zoroastrian ideal that one should be willing to sacrifice for the good of the community. However given the conditions in the world of today, when it is so difficult in a small religious community to find a suitable partner who shares one's faith, it might be worthwhile to look for other ways of attempting to preserve the faith even when marrying outside it.

ACCEPTANCE OF CONVERTS

Claiming to take Zarathustra's attitude as their model traditionalist Zoroastrians argue that Zarathustra himself did not accept converts from outside religions. Neither, they argue, should his Zoroastrian followers. They contend that religion comes directly from God and that religious faith is different from explanations about religion. For traditionalists it would be interference with God's will to convert someone to Zoroastrianism from the religion God gave them. Religion is not something someone can learn by studying. You cannot teach someone Zoroastrian religion because all religions are based on faith, and faith is God given. Modern or liberal Zoroastrians disagree. For them one can learn the basic message of Zarathustra: good thoughts, good words, and good deeds. One can change one's way of life and live in accord with Zoroastrian teachings.

Certainly a religion that has such small numbers, and numbers that are dispersed throughout the diaspora lands, runs the risk of reducing its numbers by limiting its adherents. The way to survival would be for traditionalist Zoroastrians to have large families, and traditional believers do in fact take this as their religious obligation. Yet, at least in the diaspora families who are Zoroastrian, the numbers of children are not large and adherents are not pursuing marriage at an early age. Many want to finish their education and to begin careers before they start a family.

This situation leaves Zoroastrians with another dilemma. If they want to increase their numbers they are limited by doing

At Navruz, the new year, a modern Iranian Zoroastrian family remember their dead at a cemetery in Tehran.

so in what seems the more practical way in today's world—by admitting converts. This might help to preserve the religious faith of someone who marries a person who is not a Zoroastrian. The "outsider" might well become a strong follower of Zarathustra's teachings and help raise his or her children as faithful and confirmed Zoroastrians.

This approach might also temper concerns regarding intermarriage. If Zoroastrians adhere to the long historical position that the traditionalists claim is the teaching of Zarathustra himself, the religion would remain unmixed. To follow this position

ZOROASTRIAN ASSOCIATIONS IN NORTH AMERICA AND THE YEARS THEY WERE FOUNDED

- Zoroastrian Association of America, Chicago, 1965
- Quebec, Canada, 1967
- British Columbia, Canada, 1968
- Ontario, Canada, 1971
- Greater New York, 1973
- California, 1974
- Metropolitan Chicago, 1975
- Houston, Texas, 1976
- Metropolitan Washington, D.C., 1979
- Pennsylvania and New Jersey, 1979
- California Zoroastrian Center, 1980
- Zartoshti Anjuman of Northern California, 1980
- Alberta, Canada, 1980
- Persian Zoroastrian Organization, California, 1981
- Pennsylvania, 1982
- Greater Boston Area, 1983
- Iranian Zoroastrian Association, New York, 1986
- Traditional Mazdayasni Zoroastrian Anjuman, California, 1980s
- North Texas, 1989
- Kansas, 1990
- Washington State, 1990
- Arizona, 1990
- Atlantic Canada, 1991
- Tampa Bay, Florida, 2003

would demand great sacrifices on the part of Zoroastrians; it also would not increase their numbers. No matter which road Zoroastrians choose there is a risk. One road leads to a watering down of their identity; the other risks eventual extinction.

ZOROASTRIANISM'S SUCCESS IN THE MODERN WORLD

Despite the difficulties it faces in preserving itself in the challenging modern context, the positive force of Zoroastrianism is undeniable. Both traditionalist and liberal Zoroastrians share the ethical way of the life of Zarathustra as a common inheritance. This guides them in their behavior, promotes hard work, and encourages educational excellence. These enrichments to human life defy time and place and put them in good stead in the many places Zoroastrians inhabit in this 21st-century world.

Another inheritance is found in Zoroastrians' social commitment. Zoroastrian communities stand by one another and support their members tirelessly. They provide a network for getting jobs, offer practical assistance when members of the community need it, and offer moral support in times of trial and difficulties. This practical attitude of mind can be seen in all the associations that Zoroastrians create to help one another.

Having always been a minority Zoroastrians are somewhat more at ease with small numbers than other groups might be. They are willing to go out on their own, moving to distant places to pursue job opportunities or education, trusting that they will find ways of linking up with their coreligionists. They face the modern world with a certain confidence. Zoroastrians have, as is evident from their many web pages, turned computers to their advantage. They have established networks that link coreligionists from all over the United States and Canada as well as among countries as diverse as Uzbekistan, Denmark, Australia, and Singapore.

THE CONTRIBUTION OF ZOROASTRIANISM TO THE WORLD

This religion is an important one yet so little is heard about it. As an ancient religion its teachings have influenced many other

Freddie Mercury, lead singer of the rock band Queen, was one of the most high profile Zoroastrians of modern times. He died in November 1991.

ancient religions. Many scholars have found that Zoroastrian teachings on the spirits of good and evil, heaven and hell, Satan, life after death, a Savior to come, the renewal of the world, and life everlasting have helped create the worlds of Jewish, Christian,

Islamic, and Buddhist belief. However, perhaps because this is a difficult idea for many believers to accept—that their own faith was shaped and molded by another faith—Zarathustra seems ignored, or unknown to them. And so are Zoroastrians. Zarathustra and Zoroastrianism have had much religious influence, but they have had it in a very quiet and unheralded way.

ACTION IN THE WIDER COMMUNITY

It is perhaps in their social and philanthropic work that Zoroastrians are best seen by the outside world today. In many parts

Zoroastrian priests performing a fire ceremony during a multifaith gathering hosted by the Worldwide Fund for Nature and the Alliance of Religions and Conservation to discuss environmental programs.

of India, but especially in their traditional homelands on the west coast, Zoroastrian charities, foundations, and organizations are crucial to the well-being of people regardless of creed or color. Education and health have long been traditional areas of Zoroastrian philanthropy but a new one has emerged over recent years: environmental action.

WILDLIFE PROGRAMS

The Zoroastrian outlook on their relationship with the natural world has led the community to work on forestry- and water-related issues. There is however a second reason for Zoroastrian interest in the conservation of nature. There is a need for vultures and other carrion birds to eat the dead. The rapid decline of the vultures in western India and in Iran has created serious problems for the traditional method of the disposal of the dead in the towers of silence. As a result the Zoroastrians have become among the biggest supporters of vulture breeding programs and conservation of vulture habitats in the world. And they are not just supporting those vultures near towers of silence. They are concerned with the protection of vultures worldwide as an expression of Zoroastrian commitment to the natural world and its protection.

ZOROASTRIAN TEACHINGS ON THE ENVIRONMENT

The role of humanity in the world is to serve and honor not just the Wise Lord but the Seven Bounteous Creations of the sky, water, earth, plants, animals, humankind, and fire—gifts of God on High to humanity on earth. The great strength of the Zoroastrian faith is that it cares for the physical world not merely to seek spiritual salvation, but because human beings, as the purposeful creation of God, are seen as the natural overseers of the Seven Creations. As the only conscious creation humanity has the ultimate task of caring for the universe. The faith endorses caring for the Seven Creations as part of a symbiotic relationship. Zoroastrianism sees the physical world as a natural matrix of Seven Creations in which life and growth are interdependent if harmony and perfection are the final goal. This goal is to be achieved by re-creating the primeval unity of a perfect world, unpolluted and unsullied, as was first conceived by Ahura Mazda, the Wise Lord.

In helping to bring about a state of perfection in this world and in the Seven Creations, Zarathustra enjoined his followers to tread an ethical and righteous path.

FACT FILE

Worldwide Numbers
The Zoroastrian faith is one of the oldest religions and used to be one of the most powerful. However, in recent years its number of followers has declined to around 200,000, the smallest of any main religion.

Holy Symbol
The symbol of Zoroastrianism is the *faravahar,* or *farohar,* which represents the link between the spiritual and physical worlds. The human form at the center is encircled by a ring representing the eternal soul. The wings help the soul fly upward and progress.

Holy Writings
The Avesta is the Zoroastrian holy text. It contains the Gathas, which are 17 hymns believed by many to have been written by Zarathustra, as well as observations of ritual practice and prayers.

Holy Places
Various sites in Iran, northern India, and Pakistan have great importance as the birthplaces of Zoroastrianism.

Founders
The founder of the Zoroastrian religion was the prophet Zarathustra—or Zoroaster, as the ancient Greeks called him—around 3,500 years ago.

Festivals
There are seven holy days linked with the Iranian agricultural year and seasons, the new year, and the feast of All Souls. The birth and death of Zarathustra is also celebrated.

BIBLIOGRAPHY

Boyce, Mary. *Textual Sources for the Study of Zoroastrianism.* Manchester, UK: Manchester University Press, 1984.

Breuilly, Elizabeth, Joanne O'Brien, and Martin Palmer. *Religions of the World.* New York, Checkmark Books, 2005.

Hinnells, John R. *The Zoroastrian Diaspora, Religion and Migration.* Oxford, UK: Oxford University Press, 2005.

Irani, Dinshaw. *Understanding the Gathas.* Wommelsdorf, Pa.: Ahura Publishers, Inc., 1994.

Rustomjee, Framroz. *Daily Prayers of the Zoroastrians: In English.* Colombo, Ceylon: [s.n.], 1959.

West, E. W. *Pahlavi Texts —Marvels Of Zoroastrianism.* London, UK: Hesperides Press, 2006.

Writer, Rashna. *Contemporary Zoroastrians: An Unconstructed Nation.* Lanham, Md.: University Press of America, 1994.

Zaehner, R. C. *The Dawn and Twilight of Zoroastrianism.* London, UK: Phoenix Press, 2003.

FURTHER READING

Breuilly, Elizabeth, Joanne O'Brien, and Martin Palmer. *Religions of the World*. New York: Checkmark Books, 2005.

Choksy, Jamsheed. *Evil, Good and Gender: Facets of the Feminine in Zoroastrian Religious History*. New York: Peter Lang, 2002.

Clark, Peter. *Zoroastrianism: An Introduction to an Ancient Faith*. Brighton, Eng. and Portland, Oreg.: Sussex Academic Press, 1999.

Kellens, Jean. *Essays on Zarathustra and Zoroastrianism*. Costa Mesa, Calif.: Mazda Publishers, 2000.

Masani, Rustam. *Zoroastrianism: The Religion of the Good Life (The Parsis: A Classic Collection)*. Toronto, Canada: Indigo Books, 2003.

Moulton, James, Hope. *The Treasure Of The Magi — A Study Of Modern Zoroastrianism*. Sabine Press, 2007.

Nanavutty, Piloo. *The Gathas of Zarathustra: Hymns in Praise of Wisdom*. Ahmedabad, India: Mapin Publishing, 1999.

O'Brien, Joanne and Palmer, Martin. *The Atlas of Religion*. London, UK: Earthscan, 2007.

Rivetna, Roshan, ed. *The Legacy of Zarathustra*. Hinsdale, Ill.: Federation of Zoroastrianism Associations of North America, 2002.

Waterhouse, John W. *Zoroastrianism*. London, UK: Pierides Press, 2007.

West, E. W. *Pahlavi Texts —Marvels Of Zoroastrianism*. London, UK: Hesperides Press, 2006.

Writer, Rashna. *Contemporary Zoroastrians: An Unconstructed Nation*. Lanham, Md.: University Press of America, 1994.

Zaehner, R. C. *The Dawn and Twilight of Zoroastrianism*. London, UK.: Phoenix Press, 2003.

WEB SITES

Further facts and figures, history, and current status of the religion can be found on the following Web sites:

www.avesta.org
Sacred text and other information.

www.religioustolerance.org/zoroastr.htm
A basic introduction can be found on this Web site with links to other Web sites.

www.bbc.co.uk/religion/religions/zoroastrian
Guide to the ancient religion of Zoroastrianism, including history, modern practices, beliefs, and worship.

www.zoroastrianism.com
The tenets of the religion, religious articles, and stories.

www.arcworld.org
Information on Zoroastrian teachings and environment.

GLOSSARY

Achaemenids—The rulers of the Persian Empire from 552 to 330 B.C.E.

afargan, afarganyu—A fire urn.

Afrin, afringan—A prayer invoking special blessings.

agiary—The common name for a fire temple in India.

Ahriman—The Spirit of Evil (Pahlavi).

Ahunavaiti Gatha—Gathas 28–34.

Ahura Mazda—The supreme God of Zoroastrianism. Also known as Ohrmazd, Hormazd (Pahlavi).

Ameratat—A Beneficent Immortal; the spirit of Immortality and Joy after death.

Amesha Spentas—The Beneficent Immortals, aspects of Ahura Mazda.

Angra Mainyu—The Spirit of Evil (Avestan).

Armaity—*see* SPENTA AMAITY

Asha—Truth, righteousness.

Asha Vahista—A Beneficent Immortal; the Spirit of Truth and Righteousness.

Ashem Vohu—The basic prayer of Zoroastrianism.

atash adaran—A consecrated fire temple.

atash behram—A consecrated fire temple of the highest grade.

atash dadgah—A fire temple.

Avesta—The Zoroastrian scripture.

Avestan—The ancient language in which Zoroastrian scripture is written.

Baj—The prayer before meals.

boi—The ceremony for tending the sacred fire.

Bundahishn—The Zoroastrian story of creation.

Chinvat Bridge—The "Bridge of the Separator," where souls of the dead meet judgment.

daena—Conscience; the spirit that meets a departed soul after death.

Daeva—A god of the old Iranian religion, considered evil.

dakhma—The tower of silence; a structure used for disposing of the dead.

darbe mehr, dar-e meher—A fire temple.

dastur—A Zoroastrian priest of India.

dasturan dastur—A Zoroastrian high priest (in India).

Denkard—An encyclopaedic Pahlavi work that contains a summary of the contents of the Avesta; part of the Zand.

dualism—The belief in two opposing forces, good and evil. Cosmic dualism is the belief that these two forces are part of the universe, and ethical dualism is the belief that these forces are within humankind.

Dughda—The mother of Zarathustra.

ervad—A title for a Zoroastrian priest.

faravahar (farohar)—The winged symbol of Zoroastrianism.

Frashogard, Frashokereti—The renewal at the end of the world.

fravashi—A Zoroastrian guardian spirit.

Gah, Geh—One of the five periods into which each day is divided for prayer; also, the prayer spoken at that time.

gahambar—One of six holy festivals of Zoroastrianism.

Gatha—One of 17 hymns or psalms composed by Zarathustra.

Gathic, Gathic Avestan—The language spoken by Zarathustra.

geh sarna— One of the rituals performed at the time of death.

Getig—The imperfect, physical world.

Great Avesta—The Avesta and related writings collected by the Sassanians.

Gujarati—A language of India, spoken by the Parsis.

haoma—A plant used in ancient Iranian and later Zoroastrian rituals.

haoma ritual—The principal ritual of the Yasna.

Haurvatat—A Beneficent Immortal; the spirit of Perfection and Well-being.

Hormazd—*see* AHURA MAZDA

Humata, Hukhta, Huvarshta—Good thoughts, good words, good deeds; the creed of Zoroastrianism.

jashan—The ritual of memorial and thanksgiving.

jizya—A tax levied on non-Muslims by Muslim rulers.

kai, kavi—An ancient Persian title meaning "king."

Khorda Avesta—The Zoroastrian book of daily prayers; part of the Avesta.

kusti—The sacred cord received at the initiation ceremony, which is worn around the waist as a symbol of Zoroastrianism.

Lost Avesta—Sections of the Avesta destroyed by Arab and Muslim invasions. They were reproduced in the Zand from the oral tradition.

Magi—A priestly tribe from Media in northwestern Iran.

Maidyoimaongha (Medyomah)—The prophet Zarathustra's cousin; the first person to accept Zoroastrianism.

Medes—People from Media in northwestern Iran.

Menog—The perfect stage of the world before creation of the physical world.

Mithra—An ancient Indo-Iranian god. He later became a Zoroastrian angel of the Sun's light and of Truth; one of the judges of the soul.

mobed—A title for a Zoroastrian priest.

mobed e mobedan—A Zoroastrian high priest.

navjote—The Zoroastrian initiation ceremony.

Navruz—The Zoroastrian New Year, a holy feast day.

Nyayesh—Zoroastrian prayers from the Khorda Avesta.

Ohrmazd—*see* AHURA MAZDA

Pahlavi—The Middle Persian language spoken by the Sassanians; the language of Avesta commentary.

Panchayat—The governing body of Parsis in India.

Parsi—A Zoroastrian of India.

Parthian dynasty—The Zoroastrian rulers (250 B.C.E.–226 C.E.) who began a collection of the Avesta.

Patet—The prayer of repentance.

Qajar dynasty—The Muslim dynasty that ruled Iran from 1795 to 1925.

Rashnu—The spirit of Justice; one of the judges of the soul.

Rivyats—Letters from Parsis in the Persian language to Zoroastrian priests of Iran, from the 14th to the 16th century.

sagdid—The "gaze by the dog" death ritual.

Sassanian (Sassaniad) dynasty—The dynasty (226–651 C.E.) that standardized Zoroastrian ritual and collected the Avesta.

saoshyant—The Savior to come.

Seleucid Empire—The empire established by Greek rulers after the death of Alexander.

Spenta Armaity—A Beneficent Immortal; the Spirit of Love and Devotion.

Spenta Mainyu—The holy Spirit of Truth; an aspect of Ahura Mazda.

Sraosha—The angel of obedience; one of the judges of the soul.

sudreh—The sacred undergarment received at the initiation ceremony.

Ushtavaiti Gatha—Gathas 43–46.

Vahishto Ishti Gatha—Gatha 53.

Vendidad—The section of the Avesta containing the priestly code.

Visperad—The section of the Avesta with liturgy for the holy days.

Vohu Khshathra Gatha—Gatha 51.

Vohu Mana—A Beneficent Immortal; the Spirit of the Good Mind.

Yashts—A section of the Avesta containing hymns to angels.

Yasna—The first section of the Avesta, containing the basic liturgy and the Gathas.

Yasna Haptanhaiti—A liturgy believed to have been composed by Zarathustra.

yazatas—Zoroastrian angels and holy beings.

Young Avesta—The portion of the Avesta written in the later form of Avestan.

Young Avestan—The language that replaced Gathic Avestan.

Zand (Zend)—Commentary and translations of the Avesta, written in Pahlavi.

Zarathustra—The Prophet of the Zoroastrian religion.

Zartoshti—An Iranian Zoroastrian.

Zoroaster—The Greek name for Zarathustra.

INDEX